D1825317

THE DAVID HUME INSTITUTE
THE SUNTORY-TOYOTA INTERNATIONAL CENTRE FOR
ECONOMICS AND RELATED DISCIPLINES,
LONDON SCHOOL OF ECONOMICS AND POLITICAL SCIENCE

STRATEGIES FOR HIGHER EDUCATION
The Alternative White Paper

Dedicated to the memory of
Lionel Robbins

THE DAVID HUME INSTITUTE
THE SUNTORY-TOYOTA INTERNATIONAL CENTRE FOR
ECONOMICS AND RELATED DISCIPLINES,
LONDON SCHOOL OF ECONOMICS AND POLITICAL SCIENCE

STRATEGIES FOR HIGHER EDUCATION

The Alternative White Paper

John Barnes

and

Nicholas Barr

ABERDEEN UNIVERSITY PRESS

First published 1988
Aberdeen University Press
A member of the Pergamon Group

© The David Hume Institute and
the Suntory-Toyota International Centre
for Economics and Related Disciplines,
London School of Economics
and Political Science 1988

All Rights Reserved. Except as permitted under current legislation no part of this work may be photocopied, stored in a retrieval system, published, performed in public, adapted, broadcast, recorded or reproduced in any form or by any means, without prior permission of the copyright owner. Enquiries should be addressed to Aberdeeen University Press, Farmers Hall, Aberdeen.

British Library Cataloguing in Publication Data

Barnes, John, *1937–*
    Strategies for higher education: the
    alternative white paper.
    1. Great Britain. Higher education.
    Financing
    I. Title   II. Barr, N. A. (Nicholas Adrian),
    1943–   III. David Hume Institute   IV.
    Suntory-Toyota International Centre for
    Economics and Related Disciplines   V.
    London School of Economics and Political
    Science
    379.1'18'0941

ISBN 0 08 036589 2

Contents

Foreword   vii
Acknowledgements   ix

1 Overview   1

2 The Conceptual Background   6

2.1 The Market versus the State 1: Economic Theory   6
2.2 The Market versus the State 2: Organisation
    Theory   9
2.3 Measurement Problems in Planning Higher
    Education   13

3 Current Arrangements for Funding and Managing Higher Education   16

3.1 The University Grants Committee   16
3.2 The Education Reform Act   19

4 Reform 1: Funding Students   24

4.1 Problems with the Grant System   24
4.2 Alternative Systems of Student Loans   25
4.3 National Insurance Based Loan Scheme   28

5 Reform 2: Funding and Managing Higher Education   33

5.1 The Strategy   33
5.2 The Funding of Teaching and Students   37

5.3 Financing Capital and Funding Research   39
5.4 Implications of the System   40

6 Some Specific Policy Proposals   45

6.1 The Range of Policy Choices   45
6.2 Different Models of Higher Education   47

References   51

Figures and Tables

Figure 1: Schematic Funding of Higher Education   5

Table 1: Additional National Insurance Contribution for
Each £1000 Borrowed   30

Table 2: Organisation of Higher Education: The Range
of Policy Options   46

Foreword

One of the features of the present government's policies which has perplexed many, from its loyal supporters to its severest critics, is its approach to the organisation and funding of higher education. The government has put some probing questions to the universities and the extraction of answers has made us witness to a long and often acrimonious debate, with considerable costs in time and energy for the academic profession. The government's policy conclusion is that improvement in the responsiveness of universities and other institutions of higher education to the task of maintaining and improving teaching and research standards requires tightening of centralised control of both the organisation and funding of higher education.

The reaction of many academics to this conclusion has been one of alarm. The predominant view in academic circles is that the government should think again, and there is clear support for the continuation of direct and more generous funding, with the universities remaining in the position of having wide discretion over how those funds are used. We appear to be on a collision course.

This paper by two members of the Staff of the London School of Economics and Political Science who differ considerably in their individual approach to economic and political questions seeks to resolve the funding problem in an ingenious way. Building on some previous proposals which foreshadowed the present 'showdown', they argue that universities should receive their funding directly from their 'customers'. Students would pay directly for the full cost of their education, and research would be financed largely by contracts with industry and government. Universities would then be free to make their own decisions as to the balance of their activities in the light of their ability to attract customer support.

Their proposal certainly does not require that the government withdraws completely from having anything to do with higher education. It is wholly compatible both with considerable government funding support and with government influence upon university activities. The proposal can encompass a whole range of different ways in which students could receive grant and/or loan support from government as well as from private foundations and their families. Government research contracts could embody an element of general support for pure research. The government could still regulate the 'market' including the recognition of new institutions and could insist that standards be maintained by, for example, making the appointment of external examiners an explicit condition for the award of degrees. The scheme is clearly highly flexible and its general structure is compatible with considerable variation in the amount of public intervention.

The authors make a persuasive case which, it will be noted, is based on firm evidence that the centralisation approach favoured by government would simply not achieve what the government itself is setting out to do. Their analysis of the faults of the present system alone must command wide attention, as well as their funding scheme which has the further virtue of concentrating the debate on funding where it is most needed.

Neither the David Hume Institute (DHI) nor the Suntory-Toyota International Centre for Economics and Related Disciplines (ST/ICERD), the largest research centre of the London School of Economics and Political Science, holds a collective view of any policy matter and cannot accept responsibility for the authors' statements. At the same time, they welcome this opportunity to cooperate in the presentation of what they believe is one of the most important contributions in recent years to the debate on the finance and administration of higher education. It is appropriate that the Alternative White Paper is published in Scotland. After all, it was David Hume's close friend Adam Smith who was one of the first advocates of direct funding of universities! The involvement of ST/ICERD is similarly appropriate given the LSE's central role over the years in debates about the organisation of higher education. One of its major figures, Lord Robbins, chaired the Committee on Higher Education and many at the LSE have contributed to the subject in the years since its report was published exactly 25 years ago.

Alan Peacock
Executive Director
the David Hume Institute

Nicholas Stern
Professor of Economics
London School of Economics and Chairman of ST/ICERD

Acknowledgements

To an unusual extent we are 'dwarfs riding on giants' shoulders'. Many of the ideas in this paper have a long pedigree. The notion of vouchers goes back at least to Tom Paine, and its postwar progenitors were Peacock and Wiseman (1964). The extension of the idea to funding universities via students occurred more than a decade ago to one of the authors (JB), who put the idea privately to Ministers: he found that a not dissimilar scheme suggested by Ferns (1969), had been influential in the creation of the independent University of Buckingham. Subsequently Ferns (1982) argued for all universities to be privatised, and Hills (1983 and 1988) campaigned for universities to be financed via students' fees, a view supported more recently by Kedourie (1988).

Student loans also have a long history. Income-related repayments were discussed by Prest (1966) and, in the wake of the introduction of such a scheme in Sweden in 1966, by Glennerster, Merrett and Wilson (1968). The 1960s debate is summarised by Blaug (1970, pp. 293–307), and Lord Robbins' conversion to loans is described in Robbins (1980). More recently Hills and Kelly (1988) have discussed the links between loans and decentralised funding of universities via students.

We also have many specific debts, most particularly to Professor Mervyn King. The loan scheme in section 4.3 is based almost in its entirety on ideas suggested by him, and Mark Robson helped with the computations. We are grateful to Adrian Hall and Mark Trigg for help with section 3.1 and to Iain Crawford for helpful discussion. We have received help and useful comments from Professor Mark Blaug, Professor Alan Day, Professor Meghnad Desai, Professor Howard Glennerster, Professor John Griffith, Professor George Jones, Dr Catherine Manthorpe, Professor David Martin, Professor Kenneth Minogue, Peter Muchlinski, David Walker and Dr Gail Wilson. None of them should be implicated in remaining errors, nor in the opinions expressed, for which we take sole responsibility.

An earlier version was presented at a conference on the Future Funding and Management of British Higher Education at the London School of Economics on 20 September 1988 under the auspices of the Suntory Toyota Centre for Economics and Related Disciplines.

Finally, we are grateful to Professor Sir Alan Peacock and Professor Nicholas Stern for encouragement and support of the most practical kind.

John Barnes and Nicholas Barr
London, September 1988

1 Overview

This paper is an attempt at a draft White Paper on Higher Education, drawn up in the light of the Education Reform Act and of the many changes since the publication (exactly twenty five years ago) of the Robbins Report (UK, 1963). We propose not a specific scheme, but a system which can accommodate a wide variety of different arrangements, and we seek agreement as widely as possible, both between universities and polytechnics and across political parties. We wish particularly to find areas of agreement with those who would not naturally be in sympathy with the sort of system we propose. We write as academics who have no *a priori* view in the market-versus-the-state debate, and would regard radical privatisation of the National Health Service with the same hostility that in this paper we direct at the virtual nationalisation of higher education.

Universities as a pluralist activity   In that spirit our starting point is the view that universities *par excellence* should be a private sector activity. We say this for philosophical, for economic and for practical reasons. At a philosophical level, there are good reasons for fearing any centralised control of the advancement of knowledge. The point is most easily appreciated in a pluralist society. But even in authoritarian regimes someone is needed to point out the fallibility of rulers and to play the part of the child who sees (and says) that the Emperor has no clothes. Mediaeval monarchs knew the need. In their court the jester was always allowed a good deal of licence, and was often the one person who could remind the king that he was neither omniscient nor omnipotent.

   One might imagine that these checks are not necessary in a liberal society. Even freedom-loving nations, however, can be seduced into bouts of McCarthyism. More normally they are simply the victims of fashion. The universities are not immune to this poison, but they tend also to generate the antidote. When a somewhat uncritical Keynesianism dominated the establishment, critical voices were raised in some parts of academia, which eventually promoted a reaction among younger scholars. Perpetual revisionism is the academic stock in trade.

   A second reason for criticising any attempt at centralised control of the knowledge industry relates more narrowly to economic efficiency. The Soviet Union has learned the hard way the need for free institutions to advance and disseminate knowledge if society is not to ossify and decline.

These lessons, perhaps, do not need to be learned in Britain, but it is surprising to find the government subscribing to one of the mistakes of 1960s-style planning, namely that it is possible in the medium term to identify the manpower needs of the nation (for contemporary discussion of the difficulties, see Moser and Layard (1964), Blaug (1967) and Layard (1972)). Robbins believed that manpower planning was possible only where the state controlled both demand and supply, e.g. teachers, doctors, social workers. Even that looks optimistic given demographic and technological change, wastage and changed patterns of demand. The record on teacher training, which ought to have been relatively easy to plan, has not been reassuring. In contrast, labour markets in the USA have worked well, shortages leading to a speedy increase in applicants for degrees in the relevant skills.

An even greater fallacy has crept into thinking about research, that somehow we know what is most likely to be useful to industry not just in the short run but also over the longer term. This neglect of the 'bread on the waters' aspect of the development of human knowledge will cost us dear. Rutherford foresaw no practical consequences flowing from nuclear fission; and those who developed binary mathematics in the 1860s had no inkling of the computer. More recently, catastrophe theorists were surprised to find their thinking of practical use to stock market analysts.

Even in directed economies like the Soviet Union no attempt was made to pursue only those fields of research which were self-evidently useful. The error lay elsewhere, in the supposition that only certain propositions were theoretically correct, which proved equally stifling to the advancement of knowledge. The lesson has now been learned, and Mrs Thatcher hails the advent of *glasnost* as reflecting the more enlightened ways of western society. Has she failed, however, to notice the utilitarian straitjacket which her senior civil servants have devised for the universities here?

A further criticism of unnecessary central planning is its wastefulness. When the Education Reform Bill was going through the House of Lords in June 1988, Lord Swann circulated to his colleagues some of the detailed guidelines for the allocation of research money and the control of research performance. He spoke of one document then in use, by means of which long-term contract research funding was made available. 'The document has innumerable pages. There is one page . . . [in which] you have to fill in, for the third, fourth and fifth year of your grant, what will be your quarterly expenditure under 12 different heads, and 217 little boxes must be filled out' (*Hansard* (Lords), 28 June 1988, col. 1394).

Thus can admirable intentions be translated into the worst kind of bureaucratic nonsense. Individual stupidities can always be put right but they are symptomatic of the process of creeping bureaucracy which has accompanied attempts to strengthen the planning process. Bureaucracies breed bureaucrats and spawn parallel bureaucracies in each university institution, trafficking in paper instead of ideas. The spread of reprographics makes the disease worse. Departmental meetings confront the latest questionnaires from the centre and, while they flirt with the idea of boycotting them, prudence leads them to establish plausible answers, often by way of a working party which further diverts academic effort.

The fallibilities of central planning have long been established by economists. Political scientists and organisation theorists have discovered how goals can be subverted to suit the interests of those in the organisation, and public choice theorists have reminded us that disinterested altruism is at a powerful discount where there are axes to be ground.

A decentralised system of higher education and research is thus desirable out of a philosophic belief in freedom of expression and in the interests of economic efficiency. It is desirable, in addition, to avoid the many problems of central planning. All this is well known to the government; and in search of remedies in almost every other field it has turned to decentralisation and to the market. Only in higher education does it adhere to a belief in the increasing perfectibility of central planning, a process which has continued steadily for more than a decade, culminating in the Education Reform Act.

Current problems and the proposed solution   The ill-effects are predictable. Though the government has talked of the need for diversity in funding, it has ignored the most obvious source of diversity, the student body. Its instrument, the UGC, has regulated universities as to the number of students they may admit and over the fees they may charge, and polytechnics are treated similarly. Nor will the new institutions set up by the Education Reform Act be any less constricting. Both sectors, therefore, have pursued the overseas market where constraints over price and numbers do not apply.

The single most important step towards decentralisation would be to allow institutions of higher education to charge economic fees. A further step would be to allow them to control their own numbers and, more generally, to regulate their own conduct. For this to be possible, however, higher education must be freed from direct dependence on the state. Equally, if the state is to move away from detailed control, it should no longer have a continuing and open-ended financial responsibility, but should make a finite contribution to student finance.

The obvious way to combine the state's legitimate role in influencing higher education with the freedom of individual universities and polytechnics is for the state to finance *students* rather than *institutions*. Section 5 sets out a system in which institutions of higher education charge economic fees and (possibly with some constraints) decide on student numbers. So far as teaching is concerned, institutions derive their funds mainly from students. Students are funded via a system of bursaries, backed up by a loan system: bursaries come from central government and from other sources (e.g. local government, industry); the major source of loans is the state, and section 4.3 sets out a specific loan proposal based on the national insurance system, which protects the interests of poorer students and is simultaneously compatible with public expenditure constraints. Research funding raises different issues and is discussed separately.

The system is set out schematically in Figure 1. Institutions of higher education receive income in three broad forms: fees from students; contracts for teaching and research; and endowments and other benefactions. Student fees are financed mainly by bursaries from various sources and from loans, and also (though to a lesser extent) from private resources such as earnings and from overseas. Contract income derives from various parts of government and from industry; and endowments come from alumni, industry, government and charitable foundations.

Central and local government, industry, etc. are thus able to influence the system (e.g. by establishing additional bursaries tied to particular subjects) without controlling it, and the diversity of student funding would in itself protect the independence of institutions. A system of the sort we propose establishes a meeting point between the needs of government policy and the freedom of higher education. In addition it is compatible with widely different models of higher education, ranging from the unconstrained and highly competitive to a system with a highly interventionist role for government in terms both of educational and redistributive goals.

The rest of the paper sets out our proposals in more detail. Section 2 summarises some relevant theory, and can be skipped by readers interested only in the policy proposals. In section 3 we discuss the current difficulties with funding universities and criticise the government's response, mainly in the form of the Education Reform Act. Section 4 discusses the funding of students, and sets out a specific loan proposal. Section 5 describes a decentralised system based upon student bursaries, and shows how it is compatible with virtually any view of higher education. Section 6 illustrates the point by mapping out two examples, effectively the polar opposites of a model almost entirely unconstrained by government, and another with substantial state intervention.

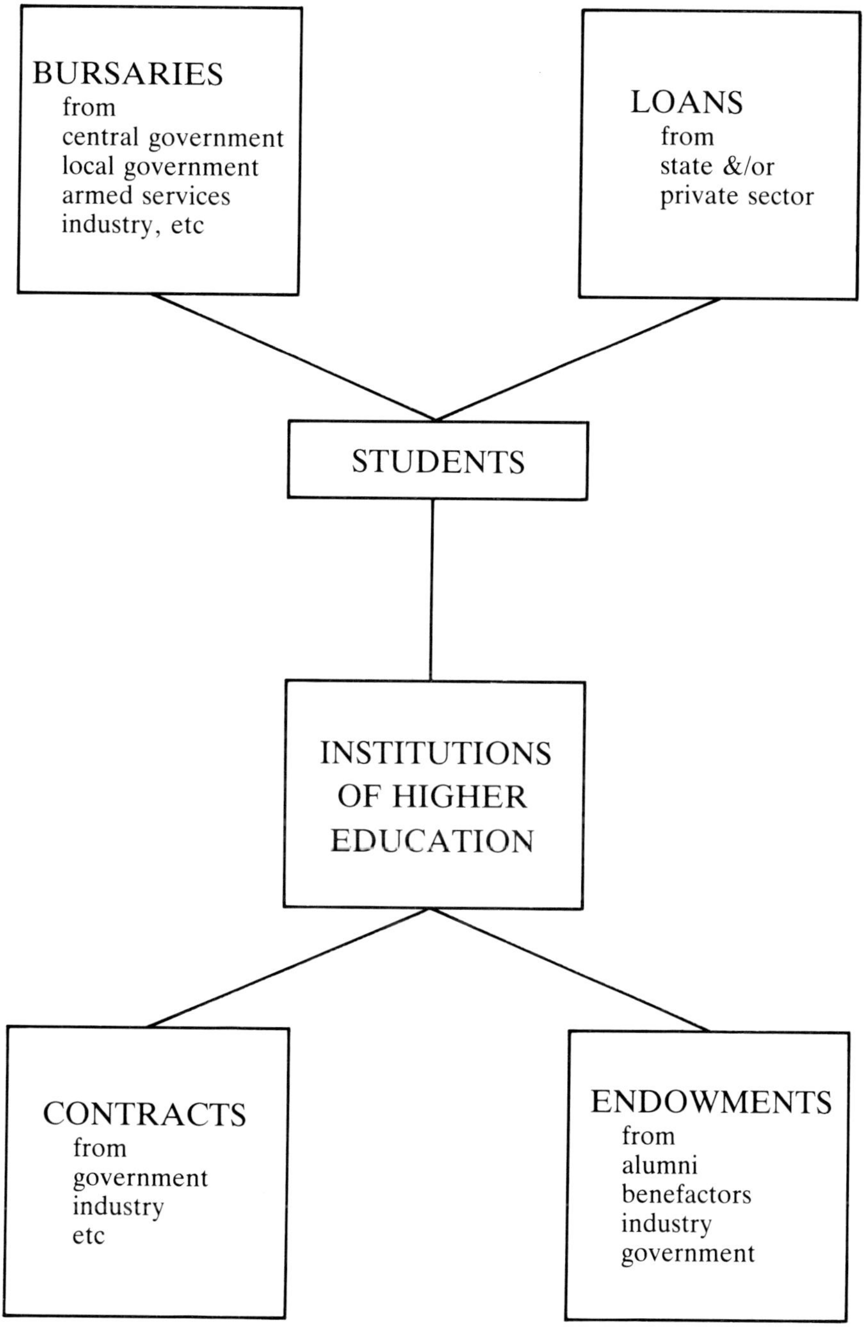

BURSARIES
from
central government
local government
armed services
industry, etc

LOANS
from
state &/or
private sector

STUDENTS

INSTITUTIONS OF HIGHER EDUCATION

CONTRACTS
from
government
industry
etc

ENDOWMENTS
from
alumni
benefactors
industry
government

Figure 1: *SCHEMATIC FUNDING OF HIGHER EDUCATION*

2   The Conceptual Background

Most of this paper is about the mechanics of present and proposed institutions. This section gives a broader context to such discussion. The argument for decentralisation of higher education rests on economic theory (section 2.1), organisation theory (section 2.2) and the measurement problems which make effective planning very difficult (section 2.3).

2.1 The Market versus the State 1: Economic Theory

It is important to distinguish the *production* of higher education from its *finance*. Production is concerned with the delivery of teaching and research, and with such issues as the public or private ownership of the capital (e.g. buildings) and, more fundamentally, whether the state or the universities makes the decisions about what level of output to produce (e.g. student numbers), what type of output (e.g. types of degree), salary structures, and so on.

Central government will continue under any feasible system to fund higher education at least in part. There is every incentive to do so since the benefits of a better-educated workforce affect a much wider group of individuals than those directly concerned. Basic research can in part be financed by firms and other private sector institutions. However, much scientific research is hugely expensive, much of the plant is used also for teaching, and industry has been reluctant to finance projects with no fairly obvious and immediate benefits. Basic research is too important to be left to the vagaries of private funding.

If the government is to meet part of the cost of higher education, it is difficult to deny it the right to influence its shape and direction. There are those who hark back to the halcyon days when the UGC allocated block grants without any attempt at interference. This route is barred for two reasons. First, the block grant mechanism was feasible during times of expansion, but is far less satisfactory when hard decisions have to be made about the allocation of increasingly scarce resources. Second, it is right that recipients of public funds should be accountable for them. The historic logic has led inexorably from the submission of university accounts (the requirement for which was introduced in 1968) to the Universities Funding Council. Some foresaw this path, and the reassurances given at the time have proved to be unrealistic. It would require a major act of abstinence on the part of government and also of the Parliamentary watchdogs to turn the clock back. This is implausible; it is also hard to justify why higher education should enjoy so unique a privilege.

That is not a case for total control, however, nor for central planning. Indeed, given the propensity of planners of all kinds to get things wrong, there is a strong case for allowing individual institutions considerable latitude in setting their own judgement against that of the government. There is a strong case also for allowing institutions to respond to the preferences of individual students; the way to reconcile the interests of government with the preferences of the consumer in this instance is through the market.

Such an approach has two sorts of advantage. First, an institution operating in a relatively free market is far more likely to be able to maintain its freedom than one substantially dependent upon a single customer who in turn offers other potential customers places at that institution 'free'.

Second, markets in this instance are likely to be more efficient than central planning. This cannot be taken for granted. The argument for a competitive market system is deceptively straightforward. According to its proponents it maximises benefits to participants in a way which the state or other allocative mechanisms cannot match. The free market is a highly efficient, self-adjusting information system: and the state has not as much information, nor an ability to acquire it as cheaply, nor a capacity to respond as quickly. Policy should therefore rely on the market system to achieve efficiency, supported by such income transfers as are thought necessary to achieve any desired distributional objective.

This argument is well known. Less widely appreciated is that its validity is hedged about by stringent conditions, including the need for markets to be genuinely competitive and, crucially, the requirement that consumers are well-informed. The case for private markets is thus valid in clearly-defined theoretical circumstances, which apply well enough in a wide variety of cases, including food, clothing and many items of every day consumption. For such commodities the costs and inefficiencies of central planning can be avoided; the idea, in peace time, of a National Food Service is quite mad.

In other areas, however, it can be argued that for technical reasons private markets will work badly, frequently because of information failures on the part of consumers and firms. Examples include both health care and medical insurance. Consumers of medical care do not (and generally cannot) have sufficient information to choose rationally; medical care is often technically complex; second opinions may be of little value if a consumer does not have adequate information to decide which opinion is correct; any information acquired is of little future use if the medical problem does not recur; and the cost of mistaken choice may be much higher and less reversible than is the case with (say) a badly chosen motor car. In addition, private medical insurance, for technical reasons, cannot cover all risks for all people, hence the major gaps in private insurance cover in the USA (see Barr, 1987, Chs 5, 12 and 13). For such reasons (which are ultimately matters of *fact* rather than ideology) it is wrong to imagine that consumers of medical care can always make efficient choices in the same way that they can (and do) with food and clothing.

There is thus a strong *efficiency* case for something along the general lines of the NHS.[1] The case for a planned system of health care, with its inevitable concomitant costs, is not that it is fully efficient, but that a market system would be even less efficient and less fair. Note however that even in the NHS most of the planning is devolved to the Regions, and the detailed planning is at District level.

An apparently different, but in many ways surprisingly similar critique of blind adherence to the simple market model is by Leibenstein (1966). His argument may be summarised as an attack on the way in which the concept of efficiency has been narrowed to allocative efficiency only, thus ignoring variations in the internal efficiency of firms. Standard price theory was a theory of markets and did not deal with intra-organisational behaviour. Managers of firms were assumed to make optimal input decisions. This view of organisational reality was, he suggested in his later (1973) article, simplistic and naive, hence his concept of X-inefficiency, which recognises that firms are organisations easily affected by sub-optimisation and goal-displacement. The similarity with earlier discussion is that the problem arises because senior managers and shareholders are imperfectly informed about the actions of those in day-to-day control.

The behaviour of organisations is discussed in section 2.2. For present purposes the key point is that universities are strongly affected by the four factors identified by Leibenstein as the main reasons for variations in cost between firms: contracts for labour are incompletely specified; the production function (i.e. the technical relationship between inputs and the resulting output) is incompletely specified or unknown; not all inputs are marketed; and if marketed they are not available on equal terms to all buyers. The most important of these factors for universities are the properly unspecific nature of their goals, the uncertain and changing environment in which they operate and the fact that part of their output, for example the transmission of culture, cannot be measured. Academics, it can be argued, should have relatively unspecific contracts, which allow them to pursue their own goals.[2]

More generally, it can be argued that the full set of activities necessary to achieve the varied goals of higher education could never be completely specified, and certainly could not be translated into individual contracts. In terms of Leibenstein's 'APQT bundle' university lecturers have great discretion over the *Activities* they will carry out, the *Pace* at which they will proceed, the *Quality* of their activities and the *Time* they will spend upon them. Close monitoring of tightly specified contracts, even if technically feasible, would be costly in real resources, would arouse hostility and lead to implementation difficulties, and raises questions of academic freedom.

Because of these difficulties, the Leibenstein arguments point to competition between universities as a relatively inexpensive way of reducing X-inefficiency. Reduction in competitive pressure clearly increases the scope for discretionary behaviour in all parts of an organisation: if there is no threat of being driven under, there is no incentive to become more efficient. The parallels with the concept of organisational slack (Cyert and March, 1963) are clear.

Higher education meets the conditions in which a market solution is likely to be efficient. This is first because consumers are reasonably well-informed: students can make sensible choices (as indeed they do already); there are effective guides to help them, and additional information can and should be provided in ways discussed later. Second, even those who run universities are necessarily imperfectly informed because of the diverse and often intangible nature of the output of higher education: detailed external planning and monitoring, in consequence, are impractical. The conclusion, on both grounds, is that competition between institutions of higher education is both possible and, in general, desirable.

The argument against central planning of higher education is not simply that it is costly and ineffective but that a market system of higher education, for the reasons given, is likely to be efficient, and therefore the costs of central planning are *unnecessary*.

2.2 The Market versus the State 2: Organisation Theory

It is useful to discuss a little more fully the way organisations behave in different environments, noting again the key role of information.

Setting goals Goals are an integral part of decision-making, but the extent to which an organisation can have a single goal or even a coherent set of goals is debatable. It is more likely that there will be multiple objectives, representing the differing aspirations of those in the organisation, and the possibility of incoherence and conflict. Organisation theorists have learned to question how far those within the organisation accept its goals, and seek to identify the informal as well as the formal organisation. Public choice theorists and those micro-economists who have turned their attention to politics show equal awareness of the process by which private goals can be substituted for publicly professed ones.

Goals are rarely as precise as theorists suppose. They may be left ambiguous quite deliberately in order to maximise support. The pursuit of excellence would be universally acknowledged as the proper goal for higher education, but it is hard to define and cannot readily be translated into operational reality. Some would claim that it is highly ambiguous, others that such ambiguity allows for diverse ways of achieving a common goal. However, it also allows lip service to be paid to the ostensible objective while very different private goals are pursued. Unless goals can be made specific it is hard to judge efficiency or effectiveness. Such specificity is hard to achieve in higher education, and the problem is compounded because many decisions are made in the face of uncertainty.

Uncertainty and the role of contracts   Several circumstances make for uncertainty. First, higher education is a complex and differentiated activity. Second, the flow of information is generally incomplete and its processing into any satisfactory form difficult. Third, the desired future state is highly debatable and cannot be other than uncertain because the future state of Britain, to say nothing of the rest of the world, is uncertain. This last problem is phrased generally; but think of the uncertainties of manpower planning, the pace with which new technologies develop and the extent to which they are breaking up traditional patterns of organisation. Fourth there is a lack of consensus about purposes and the means of achieving them. Finally, the results of the actions proposed by the new Universities Funding Council (UFC) (see section 3.2) are likely to be indeterminate, not least because their implementation will be in the hands of Vice-Chancellors, Heads of Departments, etc., whose purposes will not be identical with those of either the government or the UFC.

Lawrence and Lorsch (1967) suggest that organisations should have structural characteristics which fit the environments in which they operate. If a complex organisation is to deal successfully with a highly uncertain world, it may be best to leave many parts of its structure incompletely specified (see Loasby, 1976). Jackson (1982, pp. 144–5) makes the point succinctly:

> 'one way of viewing the set of relationships within an organisation and between an organisation and the external agents within its environment is as a set of contracts. If all contracts are rigidly specified in advance and are contingent on specific states of the world occurring with certainty, then such contracts will tend to be inappropriate and inefficient for those environments which are rapidly changing. There are a number of ways of dealing with this. Contracts could be specified in such a way that they contain a variety of clauses which become activated when certain pre-specified states of the world prevail. In such a case a single contract would be equivalent to a set of individually specified contracts.'

The cost involved in negotiating such contracts, however, would be extremely high. Buchanan and Tullock (1962) analysed the coordination problem in terms of information processing costs, which would be substantial in higher education. There is, first, the range, the complexity and the often unquantifiable nature of the data presented to central decision makers, the processing of which is costly. There is also a price in terms of time taken and missed opportunities. The process of drawing more people into the decision-making process and establishing agreement with them, would minimise the costs of imposing an unwelcome solution (which would attract covert resistance as well as overt hostility), but would introduce different costs. Finally, coordination and close supervision of contract compliance are costly and inflexible.

There is also a cost to interpreting contracts and settling disputes, and a danger of litigation, since funding is involved. At best there will be considerable diversion of effort and interruption of the smooth flow of decision-making. It is always possible to argue that more rigid contracts would be even more costly, and would have an additional penalty in the form of delay. But this misses the obvious point: even incompletely specified contracts of the kind favoured by Jackson and other theorists of bureaucracy are best avoided altogether.

Whether they operate by contract or in more authoritarian ways, excessively hierarchical organisations are inappropriate to higher education. It has been argued that hierarchies are more effective than the market (Williamson, 1975). Whatever the merits of Williamson's argument so far as business is concerned, the increasing returns from the acquisition and use of information, which he sees as justifying central planning and resource allocation, are outweighed so far as higher education is concerned by the imprecision and inadequacy of the measures available. He himself recognised the pitfalls of a purely hierarchical organisation if it grew to any size, hence his emphasis on the creation of quasi-firms accountable to a central body (Williamson, 1971). Nothing in his analysis, however, shows that this form of organisation will overcome the problems to which higher education is peculiarly vulnerable, the cumulative distortion and bias, often unintentional, which accompany the processes of filtering and interpreting information. Nor does the existence of a central planning mechanism remove the probability of lobbies and bargaining in the inevitable and continuous process of challenging and redistributing authority within the system (Krupp, 1961). No doubt if the planning organisation were able to dominate the system, it would make for stability (Arrow, 1975), but at an unacceptable price.

Hierarchical structures might be appropriate in stable environments with little uncertainty. However the world of higher education requires a more fluid structure which recognises that there may be no one best way to organise. Such a structure will be able to mobilise resources and reorganise them more speedily than any more centralised arrangement, but this requires a considerable relaxation of rules and procedures. Not only is a rigid structure unsuitable for so complex and uncertain a world as higher education; there are dangers in attempting to plan it at all.

That is not an argument for complete autonomy. Though some pluralists wish to dispense with any notion of a higher education *system,* governments are unlikely to refrain from taking an interest in the future of higher education, not least if they are expected at least partly to finance it. In the system set out in section 5, appropriate influence can be exercised without any attempt to plan higher education in detail.

Information as power   Decentralisation avoids the major danger facing even the most flexible of planning apparatuses—that referred to by March and Simon (1958) as 'uncertainty absorption'. In the process of handling information there is a tendency to portray circumstances as less complex and less uncertain than is actually the case. Information has to be simplified and summarised as it passes upward in any decision-making structure. Estimates and other forms of approximation tend to harden and paradigmatic interpretations become more rigid. Given the increasing pressures on the upper reaches of the organisation there is little time to question and reflect. Processed information is treated as more definite and more trustworthy than it is. Input from another part of the structure will be treated as given: there will be no disposition to question its status, much less its assumptions and the quality of the data and analysis used to compile it.

Note where this leaves power. As Brown (1970, p. 148) puts it

'great power is wielded by those at the point where the greatest amount of uncertainty is absorbed, since they can considerably influence the decisions that will finally be made by others. Such a position may be filled by an "expert" who is nominally quite junior in the hierarchy or by an adviser who can be appealed to on matters of difficulty that cannot be resolved by rational analysis.'

Such people, however, are not dispassionate: they too have their values and backgrounds. March and Olsen (1976) show that the particular structure adopted in complex and ambiguously-defined situations will determine which (perhaps one should say whose) skills, expertise, background, and values are brought to bear on any particular problem. The phenomenon affects not only the definition of a problem, but the structuring of the information upon which a solution will be based, and the suggestions made as to possible solutions. Pfeffer, Salancik and Leblebici (1976) go further. They suggest that it is in those fields where uncertainty is high and there are few accepted paradigms, let alone criteria, that personal influence and social relationships will have their greatest effect.

Proposition: If control of substantial amounts of information and its interpretation rest, say, with subject committees, the composition of those subject committees is likely to have a marked influence on the outcome.

Implications for higher education   The literature on organisations, as applied to higher education, suggests a paradox. In any system activities are by definition non-random. But to those who are taking part, the complexity of the whole may be too great for them to grasp all that is going on. Those who have to make the decisions will not be able to assess the full significance of what they are doing, partly because they do not and probably cannot understand all that is going on now, and partly because of the problems of predicting the future. But the major difficulty is that pointed out by Shackle (1974, p. 2) as being the human predicament:

'In order to secure its ends, choice must apply a knowledge of what will be the consequence of what. But the sequel of an action chosen by one man will be shaped by circumstance, and its circumstances will include the actions chosen now and actions to be chosen in time to come by other men. If, therefore, choice is effective, it is unpredictable and thus defeats, in some degree, the power of choice itself to secure exact ends.'

To sum up, not only is rationality bounded, which is far from unusual in decision-making, but policy is based on 'satisficing' behaviour (as Simon, 1957, characterised the process) rather than on any process of optimisation. The problems identified in the course of policy making are structured in line with the values, prejudices, and beliefs of the particular individuals currently in post. Records, rules, and precedents based on past experience condition analysis and limit solutions. Alternative considerations are filtered out (Dearborn and Simon, 1958). Given limited time and information, no attempt is made at an optimal solution. Incrementalism is the order of the day. Search procedures are inevitably heuristic and the first broadly-acceptable solution is adopted.

Organisation theory thus raises severe doubts about the effectiveness and accountability of external planning of higher education, a conclusion which accords with the economic analysis in section 2.1. The efficiency of a centrally planned system of higher education will be a good deal less than in a market system; and the risks of organisational failure are much greater than those of market failure.

2.3 Measurement Problems in Planning Higher Education

The problems of central planning of higher education are largely the result of information problems faced by decision makers. Related but separate are the problems which arise from the difficulty of measuring quantitatively many of the variables necessary for effective management. Decentralisation reduces both the scale of the problem and its importance since, in making decisions *within* an institution, it is possible to make more effective use of qualitative information.

Measuring research output Research performance, up to a point, is susceptible to quantitative measures, but it is far from clear that they tell the whole, or even the most important part, of the story. The most effective measure of quality is peer group opinion and this is prey to fashion and generational change. Retrospective judgment is usually more secure, but by definition will come too late. Seminal pieces of research can demonstrably be missed at the time of writing. Arrow's theorem, to take a noted example, has eighteenth and nineteenth century counterparts long ignored, and its immediate English counterpart, although ahead in time, attracted little contemporary attention.

There are additional problems of comparability within a subject across universities and across subjects within a university. Usefulness and relevance often cannot be determined *ex ante:* splitting the atom has already been mentioned; equally, Islamic theology became 'relevant' only after the revolution in Iran in 1978.

Measuring teaching output   In addition to research, it is necessary also to consider other outputs (better educated students), the relevant inputs (e.g. teaching) and the relation between them. None is measurable in any satisfactory way. To start with degrees, it is difficult to compare one institution with another, though the existence of the Council on National Academic Awards (CNAA) may create some comparability between polytechnics. If greater standardisation were desired, one possibility would be a national examination, along the lines of the Graduate Record Exam or its equivalents in the USA, though there would be serious problems of moderation. Such an exercise is necessary only if some form of objective performance measure is required. It is the contract system which makes these arcane problems a matter of serious debate.

Even if a satisfactory way of standardising outcomes were established, it would be a highly intractable task to relate them to the teaching a student has received. We know little of the psychological profile of the intake of particular institutions nor is there a satisfactory measure of attainment at the point of entry. Performance at 'A' level serves as a surrogate, but in the past has been poorly correlated with degree performance. With an uncertain starting line and a finishing tape which can (and on anecdotal evidence does) vary from one institution to another, any process of evaluation is on shifting sands. Since any improvement relates not only to teaching but to the student's own motivation, any input measure is doubly suspect.

Measuring teaching performance is another nightmare. There is no universally agreed typology of teaching styles, no evidence to show how they relate to effectiveness in different sizes and types of teaching arrangement, and no insight into how teaching and research interact. All told, a pretty dismal picture to which, at best, a great deal of time and research would have to be applied to achieve any satisfactory result. There must be a shrewd suspicion, however, that the main result would be a further set of questions, not least because many teachers appear to achieve their results more by the exercise of charisma or a process of osmosis than by any recognised form of teaching!

Performance indicators   Measurement problems of this sort motivate the search for simple performance indicators. Clearly there can be no objection to such indicators in principle. In using them an institution has a good sense of their context, of problems with the measures themselves and of those things they do not take into account. If, however, the measures are taken as surrogates for overall performance by those unaware of their weaknesses, they are dangerous. They must be seriously questioned when used as part of a complex mechanism for the allocation of funds. For example, they can be ambiguous. Consider telephone bills. It is by no means clear without further information whether it is good or bad to have a high phone bill; yet the size of an institution's phone bill is one of the current performance indicators.

Nor is it always clear where the balance of advantage lies: secretarial hours are easy to cut back, but the price paid by the academic community is hard to quantify. Some well-paid people will have to engage in routine chores, which hardly seems an efficient use of resources. However, providing every academic with a secretary or a personal computer might render them more 'productive', but to what end if no one could master the resulting flood of material in his or her own field? Judgments are hard to reach in such circumstances. Most local authorities have come to the conclusion that it is best if decisions are taken as close to the ground as possible, hence the local management schemes for schools and colleges in authorities like Cambridgeshire and Kent. They have now won the backing of the DES and form the staple diet of consultants' reports.

Decentralisation is the order of the day, but not apparently in higher education. Instead, the search for better and more rational decisions will lead to an endless quest for more and better information in order to check judgments and refine them. Certainly that has been the response of the University Grants Committee (UGC) to criticism of its criteria and methodology, and within institutions the response has been to construct and offer alternatives. The initiative usually comes from the administration, understandably since they are close enough to the ground to see the flaws in what the UGC has been doing but know that, if they are to continue to secure the flow of finance which their institution needs, they must make a case in terms which the UGC will understand and accept. There is an obvious temptation to find measures which put the best face on the institution.

Performance indicators can thus be ambiguous or unclear. Even worse, inappropriate indicators, by giving inappropriate incentives, can be the direct cause of inefficiency. This is a good example of Goodhart's law: identify a measure and it will inevitably become distorted. The problem is that performance indicators very rarely measure genuine performance; instead they measure that which can be measured. Measuring an institution's performance by the class of degree awarded to its students is an incentive to 'grade inflation'; measuring performance by value added is an incentive to recruit students with poor 'A' levels and to ensure that they end up with good degrees. Measuring research by the number of publications or references to them gives incentives to publish early results, and later a revised and expanded version, with the all-too-familiar explosion of journal titles.

3 Current Arrangements for Funding and Managing Higher Education

We now change gear, and turn to the practical problems of current arrangements for allocating resources to universities and polytechnics and the Education Reform Act's proposed solutions.

3.1 The University Grants Committee

THE PLANNING PROCESS

Difficulties arise in three ways — with the planning process, with the planning bodies themselves and with the outcomes of the process. The planning system, unsurprisingly given earlier discussion, is cumbersome and unlikely to be effective. Problems with financial planning, selectivity in funding, rationalisation and change and the legacy of the Jarratt Report are discussed with reference to the London School of Economics (LSE), but are shared by other institutions.

Financial planning in universities is inhibited by the demise of the old quinquennium. The UGC usually gives definite confirmation of the recurrent grant for each university only in February or March for the financial year commencing the following 1 August; provisional recurrent grant for each university is announced only some two years further ahead.

In addition, compensation from the UGC for the effect of salary awards has been inconsistent: for many years there was full compensation, but it was withheld at short notice in the case of the two-year settlement for academic and academic-related staff in 1987. Incomplete compensation, together with pay arrangements determined mainly by national negotiations over which no single institution has much control, means that institutions lack reliable forward planning information and essential control mechanisms in a key area of financial planning.

Income in the market place is, of course, also uncertain. The accuracy of forecasts depends on the quality of the forecasters, on variations in the market place (e.g. what other universities are doing) and upon unpredictable external changes (e.g. the bombing of Libya reduced the number of

American students in the UK). In a market system there are two key differences from current arrangements. First, universities *know* they face uncertainty and adopt strategies to cope; the UGC, in contrast, sets out to create an air of certainty for planners, which it then undermines by moving the goal posts (e.g. incomplete compensation for pay increases). Second, universities would have more freedom of action, e.g. borrowing money or accumulating large reserves, without the risk of losing grant.

Selectivity in funding was introduced after a huge fact-gathering exercise. Since 1 August 1986 the UGC has used a student numbers and a research selectivity model for allocating the recurrent grant. The process is complex, has numerous flaws, and produces only very crude results. In a consultative paper (UGC Circular 15/88) about the conduct of the 1989 selectivity review, the UGC admitted flaws in the earlier system. The criteria on which the work of university departments were judged ('outstanding', 'above average', 'average' or 'below average') remain unclear, while the arrangements for relating (a) judgements about academic departments to (b) the funding of UGC 'cost centres' into which these departments are (often clumsily) fitted, are obscure, sometimes muddled, and fail to take account of interdisciplinary co-operation.

The Committee appears to be unsure how to differentiate the volume of research from its quality when translating assessment of research into hard cash. As a result, the UGC is considering in the 1989 exercise asking for details of up to three publications for *every* member of the academic staff in *every* department in *every* UK university. How are these to be weighted: by publication date, length, the space accorded them for review in academic journals, peer judgement (whose?)? Serious evaluation would be a mammoth task; anything less renders the exercise valueless. Such a request is a predictable result of this kind of central planning; equally predictably, it will generate expansive mutual citations by colleagues of each other's work (another example of Goodhart's Law).

The LSE did well in the UGC's 1986 research selectivity review, but the result demonstrates the crudity of the process. The selective funding is distributed to universities by 'cost centre' — generic categories of subjects devised by the UGC. LSE's 16 academic departments cover eight UGC cost centres. Nine departments (56 per cent of its academic staff) are clustered in one cost centre; and two very small departments (some 5 per cent of its activity) each has a cost centre to itself. In the case of two departments it remains unclear what the UGC's assessment was.

Given the discussion in section 2.3 of the impossibility of measuring the quality of research none of these problems should be surprising.

The Rationalisation and Change Scheme was devised by the UGC to assist universities with restructuring to meet changed funding levels and student loads. This scheme, too, is flawed. Circulars to universities lack clarity and are prone to alter important guidance given in earlier circulars. One example in early 1987 said that new appointments would be regarded as within the scope of the Scheme, but a circular a year later said that they would probably be regarded as outside it.

The Scheme also created at least two other areas of unpredictability. Altered guidance about the level of reimbursement for restructuring under the Scheme made consistent planning at the university level more difficult than it need have been. Furthermore, there were delays in the UGC completing its consideration of universities' academic plans, approval of which was necessary before funds under the Scheme could be released. These delays reached a point in autumn 1987 where funds had to be released 'on account' pending UGC completion of its procedures. Again, these aspects could have been (and were) foreseen.

The Jarratt Report in 1985 pointed out helpful directions for universities for the achievement of efficiency, economy and effectiveness. The Report's usefulness, however, was lessened by the factors already described, which inhibited the freedom of institutions to make their own decisions. The annual reports which universities have to make to the UGC about their progress in implementing the Report's 44 recommendations represent a considerable diversion of time and effort.

THE PLANNERS AND THE OUTCOME

The UGC as a planning body is open to various criticisms. The analysis of section 2 suggests that it would never have been able to do a wholly satisfactory job, but its chances of doing so were lessened by its difficulties in recruiting good quality staff and its inadequate resources. In particular, its use of information technology was rudimentary given the scale of data processing necessary. While there is nothing wrong with contracting out *per se*, the use of Deloitte Haskins and Sells to manage the financial forecasting aspects of the 1986/7 Rationalisation and Change Scheme was evidence of the UGC's very limited in-house expertise.

Second, there has frequently been a lack of openness and accountability about UGC decisions, giving rise to suspicions, whether justified or not, that some decisions were arbitrary. In the 1986 formula, to give only one example, the Committee gave LSE only half the additional home student planning numbers requested but gave no explanation at all for its decision.

The UGC issues at least 40 Circulars to universities annually, most of them calling for some kind of response which involves the collection of information. Some requests are merely prompts to do the things which the institution should in any case be doing, but that is by no means always the case. Such information gathering is additional to the burden imposed by recent exercises concerning performance indicators, academic standards, and academic staff appraisal. At LSE alone the selectivity exercise, the rationalisation and change scheme, Jarratt and other externally imposed tasks are estimated to take up time equivalent to one full-time member of the senior administrative staff, at a full cost of around £30,000 per year. The position at other institutions is similar.

The other planners in the process are the Department of Education and Science (DES). While it is always possible to expand the numbers in a department, it is clear that with only eight civil servants in the relevant section at the rank of Principal or above, the Department cannot at present be an effective planning body for the entire higher education system. Some of the expansionist temptations which apply to a QUANGO may apply also to a government department, but a department's conduct is subject to ministerial control, and to Treasury and Parliamentary scrutiny. In sharp contrast, the UFC, is explicitly excluded from Parliamentary scrutiny and will not be allowed to publish its advice to Ministers.

The outcomes of these processes   First, it can be argued that universities are underfunded. The government argues, to the contrary, that a cartel of universities is operating, though it has found it very convenient that the UGC *de facto* controls the number of students, the funding that goes with them and the fees which universities can charge. It makes for budgetary certainty, if not for efficiency. Paradoxically, the planning process has already led to the bailing out of inefficient universities and is leading to a degree of DES accountability which Ministers may find uncomfortable.[3]

Though it is legally possible, universities have no incentive to increase home student fees. Where institutions in recent years have attempted to levy an additional charge (e.g. a college fee) over and above the standard home undergraduate fee (£578 in 1988/89), the UGC has reduced the recurrent grant by about half of the resulting extra income, with an implied threat of further action if the additional fee were not withdrawn. Matters are similar where an institution attempts to increase home student numbers. The institution gains the £578 fee, but receives no additional recurrent grant; and it remains open to the UGC, if the increase in student numbers is large or prolonged, to reduce the recurrent grant. Attempts to increase home student numbers or to raise fees thus bring in little if any additional net income.

In an important sense the main outcome of a cumbersome, complex and yet crude planning process is price control *and* quantity control. Universities can do little to affect either the number of home students they take or the price they charge. They are underfunded from public sources, and yet their hands are tied as to permissible responses.

3.2 The Education Reform Act

FUNDING

The historical background   The theoretical analysis in section 2 suggests that the problems of the UGC regime are inherent in the centralised planning exercise which it has largely become. Under the provisions of the Education Reform Act, the UGC is to be replaced by a new body, the Universities Funding Council (UFC). The new arrangements differ in many ways from the old, but two aspects predominate. First, the UGC, as its name implies, gave universities grants. Universities had to make proper use of these public funds but, nevertheless, retained considerable (though declining) discretion as to their precise use. The UFC will make contracts with individual universities, possibly in a very detailed way, possibly even on a course-by-course basis. The intention is that the contracts will specify very precisely what is to be delivered in return, thereby, it is hoped, requiring universities to act efficiently.

Second, and even more important, the UGC was set up specifically as a buffer between government and the universities to minimise any potential conflict between public funding and the independence of the universities, whereas the UFC is much more an agent of the Secretary of State for Education. The difference, however, should not be exaggerated. Though the UGC in its early days was an effective buffer, its purpose changed gradually in the wake of two developments. First, following the recommendations in the Robbins Report (UK, 1963), responsibility for the UGC passed from the Treasury to the DES in 1964; second (and probably in consequence) the Public Accounts Committee made it a condition that university accounts should be open to inspection by the Comptroller and Auditor General. Many of the fears expressed during the PAC hearings in 1966/7 (UK, 1967) have come true. Within months came the first moves by the UGC to offer more specific guidance to universities, for example on the balance between science and humanities. Still more threatening, Shirley Williams' 13 point agenda aimed at getting universities to reduce their unit costs.

While UGC guidance became more specific, it was not seen as a threat until the contraction of universities become an established government goal. The disappearance of the quinquennial grant and the cash limiting of universities, in hindsight, were stepping stones to the major cuts after 1980. At this point the UGC, whilst still offering guidance in its traditional form, became highly specific as to where the cuts should fall.

Assessment of the UFC cannot yet relate to its actual operation. But it takes little imagination to see a repetition, if not an exaggeration, of the planning problems of the last few years. First, the implementation of the contract system and monitoring compliance are likely to be a bureaucratic nightmare, compounded by the retention of the binary divide. Business could, perhaps, be conducted in a rather routine way; this will speed things up, but at the expense of the quality (or at least the quantity) of monitoring. Alternatively, contracts will be very precise and monitoring intense, though it is doubtful whether this will increase the efficiency of the outcome. In any case the process will be cumbersome, slow, highly resource intensive and, as argued earlier, largely unnecessary.

Even if sufficient resources for proper implementation were to be made available, a second problem arises, namely that the goals of the UFC are far from clear. Will it be quality alone which determines the future of particular universities and their departments, or is there to be some effort at regionalisation of student teaching? Will some institutions be encouraged or even directed to become first degree institutions, perhaps to the extent of creating first and second league institutions? Plans need clearly-defined objectives and these are usually too important to leave to the planners themselves. Manpower planning is a notoriously uncertain business. Accountants for example have a curious tendency to recruit historians, often in preference to accountants. Such inconsistencies are beyond the planner's mind.

Third, and still more worrying, is the quality of the information on which the UFC will base its judgements. The experience of the early 1980s is not reassuring. The evidence given to the Select Committee on Education and Science (UK, 1982) and bruited abroad in the press at the time of the UGC's decision to maintain the unit of resource in 1981 is entirely consistent with the predictions about oganisational behaviour in section 2.2. There is (to put it no more strongly) a suspicion that decisions were based not only on imperfect information, but reflected prejudices and *a priori* judgements thereafter clothed in the garb of rationality. Sir Edward Parkes subsequently claimed that there were in the exercise 'absolutely no value judgements about institutions'. In contrast, Ashworth (1982) alleged particular biases among the UGC assessors. Statisticians can demonstrate a lack of consistency in approach to the various universities when cuts were in train. Political scientists observed that the composition of the decision-making body seemed to have an effect on the conclusions, although the defence of those conclusions was couched always in rational terms. Kogan and Kogan (1982, pp. 106–7) tended to dismiss such criticisms in favour of charges that the UGC was simply too inexperienced and ill-equipped to do the job, but such charges were widely believed in the university world and students of decision taking are well aware of these and other obstacles to rationality.

The Education Reform Act continues the trend towards detailed central planning into which the UGC has increasingly been drawn. The resulting UFC approximates more and more closely to a state monolith, about the dangers of which the present government above all should need no reminding. They must see the consequence of the central direction of resources in the academic world: diversity, experimentation and innovation are likely to be stultified; the flexibility and freedom to respond to new opportunities will at best be constrained; long-term projects with no obvious payoff will largely cease to be funded; and the weight of demands for information, such as plans for future developments, would be even greater than under the current UGC set up.

Lord Swann, a former Vice-Chancellor of Edinburgh University, summed up as follows the effects of such arrangements (*Hansard* (Lords), 28 June 1988, cols 1394–5):

'[T]he Government intend to abandon the type of funding that has led to British universities being so highly esteemed throughout the world precisely because they have been trusted to do the best they can with only general guidance and a minimum of compulsion from government. In place of that, the Government propose an elaborate and bureaucratic system that hardly trusts anyone to do anything. . . .

'[O]ne can have only the gravest reservations about a system operated by officials in the DES and UFC that by its very nature must be bureaucratic, must be inflexible, is bound to jeopardise the freedom of research and scholarship and, by setting detailed plans if not in concrete at least in glue or treacle, cannot take account of the distinctive nature of universities.'

It is a curious paradox that a government so conscious of the dangers of ossification elsewhere should wish to impose upon those operating at the frontiers of knowledge and seeking to transmit that knowledge to their students the full rigours of central planning.

TENURE

Of the manifold implications of the Education Reform Act for institutions of higher education one more should briefly be mentioned — the vexed issue of tenure. It is possible to reach differing conclusions about its value. Later discussion (section 5.1) argues for modification of tenure rather than its abolition. No one, however, can really defend the arrangements in the Act, by which the University Commissioners are required to invalidate all contracts dated 20 November 1987 or later which offer tenure. This means that no one who did not have tenure before that date can receive it; and that anyone who already had tenure will lose it if he or she receives a new contract. The most frequent cause of a new contract is when an academic moves to another university or is promoted internally. A consequence of the Act, therefore, is that anyone who is promoted or who moves to another university after the relevant date will lose tenure. The only exception (the result of a Lords amendment) is where an academic is awarded the title but not the pay of a more senior position.

The proposal is far from fair or equitable. In addition, even in terms of the government's own objectives it is open to serious objection and is likely to prove wholly counter-productive in the short to medium term. Consider an academic who is offered promotion at his or her university or elsewhere. The government's argument is that the rewards of promotion would outweigh the consequent loss of tenure. Doubtless this is true for a 25 year old who is offered a Chair. But what about a 50 year old who is offered a Senior Lectureship? The additional income is slight, and the probability of suitable re-employment should he or she subsequently be made redundant small. Weighing the advantage of additional lifetime earnings against the loss of security, most academics in the latter part of their career are likely to stay put. Almost by definition they are members of a risk-averse profession which cares about non-pecuniary rewards and which has a rather flat career structure. Additionally, the age structure of the profession is such that there is a huge block of academics aged between 45 and 55. Thus there is a strong likelihood that many academics in the latter part of their career would refuse a new post.

Removing tenure from academics who move to another institution or who are promoted internally (unless they keep to their old pay scale), not only penalises the best academics, but gives them highly perverse incentives, and greatly hampers attempts at restructuring. There are longer-term objections. Given the existence of tenure-type arrangements throughout the English-speaking world, even (perhaps particularly) in the USA, the international competitiveness of British universities will be undermined. Consequentially, as tenure goes it will be much more costly to keep the best brains here. Tenure is a relatively cheap way of keeping them (a) here and (b) happy.

The purpose of the changes was to improve managerial flexibility (a laudable aim). If the new arrangements have genuine teeth, they are much more likely to reduce managerial flexibility, not least because UK arrangements will be so out of line with those in comparable countries; and if the new arrangements do not have teeth, nothing will be gained managerially. A possible solution is suggested in section 5.1.

4 Reform 1: Funding Students

This section starts with an analysis of the current grant system, and proceeds to a discussion in section 4.2 of different types of loan. A specific loan scheme is advocated in section 4.3.

4.1 Problems with the Grant System

The UK system of financing students by way of grants looks less rosy today than in the first flush of the Robbins expansion. Even then it attracted criticism because it relied on the parental contribution to top up the grant. No government, however, has been willing to implement the recommendation of the Anderson Committee (UK, 1960) that grants should be wholly state financed. The grant today is even further from providing full maintenance (Barr and Low, 1988; Moore and Roberts, 1988), even when the parental contribution is included. The DES admitted to the Select Committee on Education that 'we would no longer maintain that the maintenance element of the mandatory award is sufficient to meet all the essential expenditure of the average student' (*The Times*, 3 December 1986, p. 5).

Many students do not receive even this reduced amount, however. In 1982/3 40 per cent of students received less in grant and parental contribution than they should according to the rules of the grant system. The average shortfall for each student in deficit was about 14 per cent of the full grant. Even when income from all sources (e.g. including the student's earnings) is taken into account, one student in eight received less than the grant system says he or she should.

Thus the grant system, judged in its own terms, does not perform very well. As a result, even taking all sources of income into account, one student in 13 in 1982/3 was below the long-term supplementary benefit level. There is no reason to believe that this situation has changed for the better, rather the contrary. The main reason for these deficits (and in itself another problem with the grant system) is the failure of the parental contribution system. Of those students who should have received a parental contribution only half received the full amount; the remainder received on average only £53 of every £100 of assessed contribution (Barr and Low, 1988, pp. 31–6).

The deficiencies in the parental contribution system render it universally unpopular, contribute to poverty among students and deter an unknown number from applying in the first place. In addition, there is solid anecdotal evidence of students with a substantial shortfall in parental contributions working long hours to earn money, at the expense of the quality of their degree. This is inefficient, in that it distorts the division between studying and earning which a student would choose with a larger grant or in the presence of a sensible loan system.

Though students are often poor their parents are not, since the majority of students come from middle-class backgrounds. A further problem with the system, therefore, is that it disproportionately benefits students from better-off families. Compared with the population at large, students are twice as likely to come from higher-income families (the top 40 per cent of incomes), and over three times as likely to come from those with the highest incomes (roughly the top 12½ per cent of incomes). Students at Oxford and Cambridge are 2½ times as likely to come from a higher income family, and nearly four times as likely to come from one in the highest income ranges (Barr and Low, 1988, pp. 49–59).

Finally, the grant system is expensive, making it difficult to expand the higher education system. Thus the UK has relatively few students; in the USA, Japan and Germany, for instance, between two and three times as many people from the relevant age group go to university.

4.2 Alternative Systems of Student Loans

It is possible (Hills, 1988; Hills and Kelly, 1988) to link student loans and student finance of higher education in a logical and coherent structure. There are strong attractions to doing so, but it is important to be clear that the two issues are separable. Loans can be combined with the present system of university finance and its prospective successor. Equally, the government could fund students in whole or in part without resorting to loans, but university fees could be raised to economic levels.

The loans strategy A partial switch to loans could increase efficiency in at least three ways. First, higher education benefits society as a whole, and it therefore aids the efficient allocation of resources if the state pays part of the cost. However, a degree also confers private benefits on students (higher pay, greater job satisfaction), and so it is both efficient and equitable if students pay part of the cost themselves.

Second, is the issue of capital markets. If capital markets were perfect (i.e. if all students could borrow against their future earnings) the private market could supply loans itself. Since many students are not able to obtain long-term private loans, government intervention is necessary, either to guarantee private loans or to provide loans itself.

Third, loans reduce the public costs of higher education, making it easier to expand the system to a larger and (it can be argued) more efficient size.

Loans, additionally, can have equity advantages. They reverse the tendency of the grant system disproportionately to benefit the better off. They reduce the public cost of higher education and so would make it easier to pay grants to 16–18 year olds, which is where the main bottleneck occurs in the progress of children from poorer backgrounds towards higher education. Finally, it would be possible to replace parental contributions by a loan system, a desirable objective given all their problems. It is desirable also because the idea of taxing the parents of academically successful children is bizarre; it makes much more sense to give the children access to their own future earnings and then later to tax the *children*.

Debate about loans has been bedevilled by confusion over different types of scheme. The distinction between *commercial loans* (which may or may not have a subsidised interest rate) and *income-related loans* (where repayment is based on a student's subsequent income) cannot be over-emphasised. Critics of loans invariably attack the former, as though no other way of organising loans existed. This section argues that loans with income-related repayments are the productive way forward.

Commercial loans resemble a mortgage. Repayment is related to the size of the loan, to the interest rate and to the speed with which the loan is repaid. There are major arguments against commercial loans as the primary source of undergraduate finance (though, in many cases, it may be the more useful approach for graduate study).

The first problem is practical. Many students would not be able to obtain a long-term loan from a bank or building society. The apparent solution is for the government to offer a loan guarantee, thus increasing the amount of money in students' pockets without raising public spending. This line of argument is a mirage for at least three reasons. The first is purely technical: Treasury rules require the *whole* of the guaranteed sum to be added to public expenditure.

Second, even if the rule were relaxed, commercial loans would still involve considerable public spending. Financial markets for student loans do not work well; doing a degree, for the reasons discussed shortly, is risky; in addition, there is no collateral (slavery being illegal). Thus banks will not be prepared to offer large, long-term loans to students without a Treasury subsidy on interest rates (extra public spending) and a Treasury guarantee. Given the degree of riskiness, the Treasury guarantee will not be a mere fiction, but will be costly (in the USA the default rate is currently running at about 14 per cent of outstanding loans, and a total deficit of approaching $5 billion).

Third, because of the cost of subsidies and loan guarantees, the Treasury will impose stringent controls on the total amount of loan guaranteed. There will be a battle every time it is proposed to raise the amount a student can borrow or to extend the range of students eligible. The point is acutely relevant to those currently in receipt of non-mandatory awards, whose size and number have been constricted by pressures on local revenues. Second qualifications and further professional training are usually financed by such awards, and there is a strong case for helping mature students and those in need of retraining. In sum, it is a myth to assume that commercial loans do not involve added public spending. They are costly and on that account the system is not readily extensible.

An additional, and fundamental, problem arises on the demand side. Commercial loans are inefficient: they waste talent if they deter able but impoverished young people from embarking on higher education; they reduce inter-generational mobility; and they may create artificial scarcities in certain occupations, resulting in surges in pay. Furthermore, they do nothing to eliminate the parental contribution.

It is sometimes pointed out that people from the lower socioeconomic groups will take out a mortgage to buy a house, so why would they not borrow to buy a degree? The analogy is wholly inapplicable. In addition to the tax advantages for house purchase, when someone buys a house (a) he knows what he is buying (because he has lived in a house all his life), (b) the house is unlikely to fall down, and (c) he has a fairly good idea that the value of the house is likely to appreciate. When someone borrows to buy a degree (a) he is not fully certain what he is buying (particularly if from a family with no degree holders), (b) there is a high risk (or at least a perceived high risk) of failing the degree outright; and (c) not all degrees are going to be rewarded as expected over a lifetime, because fashions and employment prospects can change. For all these reasons borrowing to buy a degree is considerably more risky than borrowing to buy a house, and the risks are likely to be greater for those from a poorer background and for women.

Commercial loans have other problems. The default rate, as discussed earlier, is likely to be substantial. In addition, they are unpopular for at least two reasons with the banks who would have to operate them. First, they will be costly to administer. Second, students have threatened to boycott commercial banks which participate in a government loan scheme. In the past, banks could shrug off such threats. Now that building societies have joined the clearing system, however, banks fear an exodus of student accounts to building societies.

Loans with income-related repayments organised, for instance, via the tax system once a student has finished his or her degree, are automatically related to ability to pay.[5] Such loans have major advantages. Students pay part of the cost of their degree themselves, which is both efficient and fair. The scheme resolves the worst problems of capital market imperfections. In the long run (though not necessarily in the short run) the public cost of expanding higher education is reduced. The scheme limits the extent to which the better-off benefit most from the grant system. It solves the problem of unpaid parental contributions, thereby improving access to higher education for those people (often women or mature students) whose parents do not pay the assessed amount. In the long run the approach could increase equality of opportunity by using saved public spending to finance grants to 16–18 year olds. In short, such a scheme would make access to higher education easier for students from poor backgrounds. For these and other reasons

> 'virtually every advocate of student loans in Britain (Alan Peacock, Jack Wiseman, Alan Prest, Sir Charles Carter, Gareth Williams, Ernest Rudd, Anthony Flew, Donald Mackay, Michael Crew, Alistair Young, Arthur Seldon, Lord Robbins and Mark Blaug) . . . favours an income-related loans scheme . . . and not a personal loan repayable in a fixed number of years after taking up employment' (Blaug, 1980, p. 45).

The choice of repayment model has relevance not only to a student's access to higher education but also to his or her subsequent career. Harvard Law School has an income-related loan scheme which enables its graduates to go into community service, an option largely foreclosed by the need to repay a large commercial loan. Income-related repayments are thus arguably more efficient (given a world which departs from the competitive ideal), in that they distort job choices less than commercial loans.

Not least because of these advantages a number of such schemes exist or are under discussion. The Swedish government introduced a scheme in 1966 by the simple expedient of freezing the grant. Fees continued to be publicly funded for all students, and the grant was topped up by a loan from the state, with repayments related to subsequent income, and with additional assistance for students from disadvantaged backgrounds. A scheme to be introduced in Australia on 1 January 1989 will recoup part of the cost of higher education by imposing an additional one per cent income tax on graduates with above average earnings, rising to 3 per cent for those on the highest incomes.

The present government, it is fair to say, has not made distributional goals its primary objective. It has, however, stressed fairness and independence; and a better-educated workforce is likely to raise national wealth. Helping people to progress educationally accords with both objectives: commercial loans do little to help; loans with income-related repayments make a considerable contribution. They should be adopted for two reasons: they foster intergenerational mobility; and they give people training (cf the various job training schemes).

4.3 A National Insurance Based Loan Scheme[4]

This section advocates a specific loan scheme with repayments related to a student's subsequent income, which can be phased in without even the short-run necessity for an increase in public spending. Though the idea of income-related loans is old, the mechanism suggested here is new.

The idea   Repayments should be based on earnings rather than a student's total income (which includes investment income), because it is earnings which are increased by having a degree, and also because it would be an administrative nightmare to withhold tax on investment income at a different rate for graduates than for others. Repayments should also be finite. If they were (say) 2 per cent of taxable income for life, Mick Jagger (one and a bit years as an LSE undergraduate) could end up financing more or less the whole system of UK student support. Repayment can be limited by paying a percentage of all earnings until the loan is paid off, or by paying for life, but only on a band of income.

A natural way of meeting both requirements is for students to take out loans from the state, and to make repayments in the form of a graduate addition to the National Insurance Contribution (NIC). This, it turns out, is feasible for quite a modest increase in NICs.

What is more, for a given student population, the scheme can be introduced without the necessity for any increase in public spending. The starting point is to set the level of next year's grant in the usual way, and initially to keep in place the system of parental contributions. In addition, announce two changes: that henceforth 10 per cent of the grant, the percentage rising over time, will be repayable via an addition to NICs; and that the parental contribution will be phased out as rising repayments make it possible to do so without increasing public spending. The system thus costs the same as current arrangements for about three years, at which point repayment revenues start to come in.

The arithmetic of the scheme suggests that it is feasible for a relatively small increase in NICs. Table 1 shows the extra contribution to repay a £1,000 loan under different assumptions. With a 5 per cent interest rate, for example, an individual with national average earnings can repay a £1,000 loan over 25 years with an additional NIC of 0.6 pence per pound, i.e. by paying contributions at 9.6 per cent of earnings rather than the current rate of 9 per cent.

It is plausible to assume that most graduates will have at least national average earnings over the course of their working lives. Suppose, for simplicity, that the grant is £2,500. At a 5 per cent interest rate, half the grant for a three year degree could be repaid over 25 years by an additional NIC of 2¼ pence per pound of earnings. At a 7½ per cent interest rate (roughly the mortgage rate after tax) the extra NIC would be 2¾ per cent. It would thus be possible to abolish parental contributions (which average almost half the full grant) at no public cost with an extra NIC of around 2½ per cent of earnings for the typical student. If graduates command salaries at or above the upper earnings limit, half the grant could be repaid at an

Table 1:   ADDITIONAL NATIONAL INSURANCE CONTRIBUTION
(pence per £1) FOR EACH £1000 BORROWED[a]

	10 years	15 years	20 years	25 years
5% interest rate				
£6000[b] per year	2.11	1.57	1.31	1.16
£11,648[c] per year	1.09	0.81	0.67	0.60
£15,860[d] per year	0.80	0.59	0.49	0.44
7½% interest rate				
£6000[b] per year	2.35	1.83	1.58	1.45
£11,648[c] per year	1.21	0.94	0.81	0.74
£15,860[d] per year	0.89	0.69	0.60	0.55
10% interest rate				
£6000[b] per year	2.60	2.10	1.87	1.76
£11,648[c] per year	1.34	1.08	0.97	0.90
£15,860[d] per year	0.98	0.79	0.71	0.66

NOTES: [a] Per £1000 borrowed; compound, monthly repayments
[b] £6000 = approximately half of national average earnings
[c] £11,648 = national average earnings
[d] £15,860 = upper earnings limit for national insurance contributions

interest rate of 7½ per cent by a 2 per cent additional contribution.

There are other possibilities. The extra contribution could be paid until the loan has been paid off, or for life: the former relates contribution more strictly to benefit, the latter is more redistributive. Either is defensible; neither raises administrative problems. It would also be possible to share the additional cost between employer and employee, not least to economise on skilled personnel in the context of a declining number of young people. If repayment were over the whole working life, half the grant could be replaced by an extra NIC of 1 per cent each for employee and employer, i.e. a 'penny in the pound' scheme.

In the longer term, once the system is well-established, it could be extended to cover a larger proportion of the grant. Assuming national average earnings, a 5 per cent interest rate and repayment over 25 years, the entire grant could be replaced by an additional NIC of 2¼ per cent of earnings each for employer and employee. The maximum annual repayment (for someone at the upper earnings limit) would be just over £350 per year, with a similar payment by the employer. Someone earning £6,000 per year would repay £11.25 per month. Readers can make their own assumptions and use the figures in Table 1 to devise their own scheme.

Advantages The scheme has very major advantages over the current system and also over the various loans schemes already considered. The inefficient and highly unpopular parental contribution could be phased out; the phasing out can be achieved without any increase in public spending; and the process could be accelerated as public expenditure constraints permitted, if the government so wished.

There are other advantages. Since the student benefits from having a degree, it is right that he or she should contribute towards its costs; and, like any loan scheme, the one suggested here reduces the extent to which students from better-off families benefit disproportionately from the grant system. Furthermore, repayments based on national insurance are related to the student's subsequent income. Someone who is unemployed makes no repayments whilst he or she is unemployed; and a graduate nurse pays back very little, at least early in her career. Both features are crucial to the efficiency and equity, and also to the political acceptability, of any substantial reliance on loans.

The scheme causes no major administrative problems. All students have a National Insurance number already or could easily obtain one. The scheme requires no separate legislation, but only the insertion of the relevant clauses into the Finance Bill. Furthermore, the scheme would be cheap to implement and bad debts would be minimal (for the contrast with US arrangements, see Underwood, forthcoming). Individuals have neither the opportunity to evade NICs on any substantial scale nor, importantly, any incentive to do so, since evasion affects future benefit entitlement. Since the additional contribution is small, it is unlikely *per se* to cause emigration; and in the unlikely event that emigration caused problems, government (except for students who emigrate upon graduation) has the individual's past contributions and his/her future benefits as security.

The use of NICs has additional advantages when compared with repayments via the income tax system, of the sort incorporated in the new Australian scheme. Unlike income tax, repayments via NICs are based on earnings but, appropriately, not on investment income. They also solve the 'Mick Jagger' problem referred to earlier; for those above the upper earnings limit the additional NIC is equivalent to a lump sum tax, with the important efficiency advantage that it will not distort the choice between jobs. Repayments are levied on an individual basis, and so there is no problem of husbands being asked to repay the loans of non-working graduate wives; thus they solve automatically the so-called 'negative dowry' problem. They also lend themselves readily to an employer contribution.

It has been suggested in a British context that the Inland Revenue is very reluctant to administer a scheme based on income tax. In contrast, the national insurance mechanism is absolutely the right vehicle for repayments. The former student is paying for part of his or her degree, and so repayment properly takes the form of a contribution, which is an important aspect of national insurance. People already pay contributions for a future benefit like pensions; here they pay a contribution for a past benefit. The principle is entirely the same: in both cases national insurance enables an individual to redistribute income over his or her lifetime. The resulting system is also a form of group insurance: the risk of borrowing to finance a degree is taken on by the generation of graduates as a whole, rather than by individual students, who are protected against unemployment and other contingencies. Since there are technical problems with private insurance for risks like unemployment (Barr, 1987, Ch. 8), it is *efficient* as well as equitable for the state to organise student loans in this way.

The government should implement a scheme along these lines as a matter of urgency.

5 Reform 2: Funding and Managing Higher Education

5.1 The Strategy

While the proposals on loans are definite and specific, this section is more broad-ranging. It sets out a system for funding higher education which accommodates a wide range of possibilities. It is compatible at one end of the spectrum with a relationship between government and the universities similar to that which currently exists; at the other is a set of autonomous institutions in full competition with each other. The system proposed here is compatible with either extreme, or with anywhere in between. Section 5.1 outlines the strategy, sections 5.2 and 5.3 look in more detail at the funding of teaching and research, respectively, and section 5.4 discusses the implications of the resulting system.

Blind alleys The arguments of sections 2 and 3, suggest that central planning is wholly inappropriate to higher education. Instead of persisting with such a mechanism, the government should make a fresh start. It should allow higher education institutions to manage themselves within a framework which safeguards academic freedom but which subjects them to scrutiny to prevent concealment of poor teaching or low academic standards.

In the light of earlier discussion two solutions should be ruled out. Desirable though the idea might appear, a return to largely unconstrained block grants and quinquennial planning is a non-starter. As history has shown, the pressure for accountability for public funds leads inevitably to substantial intervention and eventually to a planning system of the sort we have currently. At least as important, the block grant mechanism does not lend itself to times of resource constraint, because it offers no way of making hard choices (the Cardiff incident is a good example).

The second so-called solution is the idea of a series of contracts, some specific and others more generally related to teaching and research. This is the model implicit in the Education Reform Act, whose difficulties were discussed at length in section 3. They result in a quasi-political bargaining process in which the actual performance of institutions is subordinated to perceptions of that performance, which may be distorted or wholly mistaken. The record of the UGC in this respect has not been reassuring. This is not a matter for blame; it is an inevitable consequence of attempts at strategic planning in conditions of uncertainty and with very imperfect information.

In addition to the practical difficulties inherent in strategic planning through contracts, there are objections from those who see in it a threat to academic freedom (Griffith, 1987). It is difficult to see how contracts are compatible with the degree of autonomy appropriate to universities. The relationship between institutions of higher education and the new funding councils, whatever the intention, will not be between equals but that between paymaster and servant. The contrast with the government's wish to diversify the source of research funds is obvious.

The reasons why the UGC was compelled to take on its present character were discussed in section 3.2. Present arrangements rightly find little favour with government or the universities. The latter see it as the government's agent for imposing financial restrictions on higher education. The government regards it as a cartel, disliked by universities because it safeguards the general interest of the producers of higher education at the expense of particular interests. However the UGC has not prevented the need for government to step in, as at Cardiff, and spend money for which it must account to the Public Accounts Committee. The UGC, in the government's eyes, lacked the ruthlessness necessary to enforce efficiency. The UFC, however, is not so different and is unlikely to fare differently, disliked by government because it has 'gone native' and hated by the universities because the reasons for its decisions do not bear close scrutiny.

Phasing in fee bursaries   The first step towards breaking the cartel is for university fees to be raised. Institutions already have the legal power to do this, but no incentive if the UFC's response is to cut other funding and to maintain control over home student numbers. The government should take the initiative and set fees at an economic level, with different fees for arts, science and medicine. The fees would cover teaching costs plus a proper contribution to administrative overheads, but no attempt should be made to recoup any of the costs of research. The gain for higher education institutions is obvious: they will be less dependent on the funding councils. The benefits to government are less clear, unless the step is the first of several towards a freer system of funding. Institutions would compete for a declining number of young people and would seek to extend access to higher education. The government, however, has to ensure that competition between institutions ensures not only responsiveness to student demand but a genuine and sustained desire to minimise costs, and to improve efficiency and quality. If this is done, there are real gains for the government.

The major route for public funding of higher education should be through student bursaries. Institutions should be free eventually to set their own fee structure for home and overseas students, with no control over the numbers they recruit. If the government is to impose limits it should be in a manner compatible with the new system of funding, i.e. by restricting the number of publicly-funded bursaries which any one institution might receive. We return later to this point.

It is possible to move immediately to the current overseas fee level; but it would be wise thereafter to phase in moves towards total autonomy in setting fees. Institutions should be permitted to depart from the fee levels stipulated by government on the basis of a crawling peg system, and the permissible gap could be widened over time to the point where the pegs were largely redundant. The incentive for institutions to conform with this regime would be the continuation of an element of recurrent grant for a number of years, as argued below, to finance basic research while endowment income builds up. It would be open to an institution to waive its right to recurrent grant in return for full control of its fee structure. Whether in the long run the state should set maxima and minima is a matter for debate, though, in general, control of fee levels is undesirable if institutions are to be responsible and accountable for their own decisions.

Part of the additional fee income could be devoted, if the institution so wished, to accumulating its own scholarship fund, and it would be open to the government to offer inducements to that end. It has been suggested that it is already open to institutions to use this route to break free of the cartel, but the ability to raise fees sufficiently to create such room for manoeuvre is limited by the immediate penalties likely to be imposed. Only the most prestigious institutions could face such a step, and they have little incentive to do so.

Management powers   As well as fees, an institution would determine the salaries, terms of service, and possibly also the pension rights of its staff members. The government should vest all the existing assets of an institution in that institution, and should confer on it the full power to patent, lease, sell or otherwise derive a revenue from the scholarly work of its members in accordance with their individual contracts. Each institution would be treated as a charity, and the tax regime should be supportive of donations.

One aspect of terms of service is tenure. The Education Reform Act establishes Commissioners, one of whose tasks is to inspect the statutes of individual universities, and to disallow tenured contracts entered into after 20 November 1987, with the likely ill-effects described in section 3.2. Such a *dirigiste* approach could not coexist with the proposals made here. In an internationally competitive world, tenure is one of the weapons which UK institutions will want to have in their recruitment lockers, its nature and extent being a matter for each institution to determine in accordance with its own particular needs.

The experience of the great private universities in the USA offers valuable lessons. The detailed provisions vary, and the characterisation below is an amalgam which draws on the spirit of US arrangements. The starting point is that tenure exists and is taken very seriously. But it is qualified in three important ways which are directly relevant to the UK. Tenure, first, should be hard to get, and should generally come rather later in a career than has been the typical experience at many UK universities. Second, dismissal for good cause, though subject to stringent procedural safeguards, should have very much stronger teeth than current arrangements. Third, given the moves towards a market system, the validity of a tenured contract should be qualified if the institution were to go or be going bankrupt. Tenure, modified so as to be breakable if an entire department or university is to be closed, accords closely with what occurs at private American universities.

Control of courses and safeguards   Courses, their length, content and methods of study would be controlled by the institution. There would, however, be safeguards. First, and as a bare minimum, there should be statutory provision for a rigorous system of external examiners, whose final reports would be public documents.

Second, consumers must have sufficient information to make rational choices. Institutions should publish relevant data and there should be an equivalent to the Director of Fair Trading to monitor them and prevent them from being fudged. One possibility is a small efficiency audit unit, possibly attached to a Joint Select Committee of both Houses of Parliament and making regular reports to it. While some will see such a body as continuing centralisation, some policing of markets has major advantages in terms of ensuring accurate information. Once such institutions exist it is likely that they will be buttressed by private agencies. The growth of a 'good university guide' industry is predictable and, given that the raw data are accurate, desirable.

Third, and more contentious, is the possibility of an external monitoring and assessment body. If there is to be one (and there is growing pressure for some external guarantee of academic standards) something along the lines of H.M. Inspectorate would be desirable, with powers of publication but not of direction. Polytechnics and Colleges have always been subject to such reports and, until recent changes, have had also to secure validation of their courses from the CNAA, which has powers of direction. Arguably the best guarantee of successful institutions is a continuing flow of applicants, but published reviews, particularly of teaching (as occurs already with University Education Departments), seem highly desirable. The French and the Dutch are proceeding on similar lines.

It is essential that all these forms of information are accurate and up-to-date, otherwise competition could lead to a degradation of standards. The purpose of the safeguards, it should be stressed, is to ensure educational due process, *not* to act as censors or thought police. The sanction on institutions should be publication of reports, not direction. There is a risk of apparent contradiction with earlier criticisms of performance indicators But judgements are already being made on the basis of formal and informal information, which should therefore be extended and verified. In the system suggested here, judgements will be made by individual students, and none will carry massive financial consequences; the process would be cumulative, but institutions would have a chance to respond to correct both misinformation and poor performance.

A further aspect of these safeguards relates to the establishment of new institutions of higher education. The struggle to establish the University of Buckingham is recounted by Peacock (1986) and shows how exclusive the present system is. It is perfectly possible to safeguard standards whilst reducing barriers to entry. It should be open to any group of individuals to establish a new institution and to offer to teach courses to any students prepared to pay for them. Such institutions, however, would not be able to confer properly validated degrees, nor to accept students funded by state bursaries unless it was recognised as a properly constituted university. The initial step in seeking such recognition would be to accept the various safeguards outlined above. The institution would then be eligible to apply for recognition to the Joint Select Committee. The Committee would not be empowered to confer university status, but it would be the appropriate all-party forum to make a recommendation to the Secretary of State.

Consumer choice clearly plays a key role. The crucial assumption is that potential students can make rational choices or that they have surrogates who can do so on their behalf. The operation of the present UCCA scheme and the fact that potential students already have strategies for coping with oversubscription, universities which insist on being the first choice and the like, suggest that students are well-informed, likely to become more so, and well able to make sensible choices about institutions and courses. It is already the case that students can turn to various publications to assist in their decisions; and sixth form career conventions are generally well-attended and provoke intelligent questioning. In addition, the safeguards just discussed would generate precisely the sort of information students need.

5.2 The Funding of Teaching and Students

The outlines of the system should now be clear: institutions would decide on desired student numbers, on the courses they offered and on fee levels; students would apply to their chosen course, given the multiple sources of information on course content and quality, and the various safeguards. So far as their teaching and related administrative activities are concerned, universities would be fully funded by students' fees.

Though the extent to which the government makes itself responsible for student fees and maintenance is a question which is in principle separable from the funding of higher education, it is useful to discuss the topic at this stage.

Numbers of state-supported students   The government would issue state bursaries, generally linked to 'A' level performance and the willingness of a university to admit. The Treasury would not tolerate, nor should it, an open-ended commitment based simply on the fact that a student had been admitted to a particular institution. The temptation to lower entrance standards to attract additional state funds is too obvious to need elaboration. Reliance on minimum levels of performance coupled with the offer of a place in higher education will produce a finite number of candidates for state bursaries and one which is reasonably predictable from year to year. For the sake of argument the state might offer bursaries to all students who achieve two C passes or three Ds, or to those who achieve a minimum number of points, using the scores familiar to those who deal with university entrance.

It is desirable that an increasing number of mature students, not all of them formally qualified for entrance, should proceed to higher education. There should be additional bursaries for such students. They could be awarded on a first-come, first-served basis, or attached to particular institutions known for their expertise in handling such students. These suggestions are not mutually exclusive.

The level of student support   The bursary should, in the first instance, cover fees on a non-means-tested basis and also maintenance broadly at the level of the present grant, and means tested as currently. Fee bursaries should remain a feature of the long-term landscape. The maintenance element should be phased out in whole or in part, and the entire system backed by a loan scheme to make up any shortfall and also to fund students who fancied their chances but who had been unable to obtain a bursary.

The crucial distinction between commercial loans and loans repayable through the tax or national insurance system has already been stressed. The case for a national-insurance-based system was made in section 4.3. At this stage it is necessary only to set out the key conclusions. First, loans raise not a two-way debate (i.e. bursaries versus loans), but a three-way debate (bursaries, commercial loans and loans with income-related repayments). Second, any loan scheme should be phased in over a period of years to give people time to adjust and, importantly, also to control the impact on public expenditure.

Any system of loans will have distributional effects. An obvious question is the effect on students from poorer backgrounds if better universities charge higher than average tuition fees. Viewed in one way higher fees reflect higher quality, for which people should be prepared to pay; we do not, after all, worry unduly if smoked salmon costs more than corned beef. Alternatively, one might wish to take deliberate action to increase equality of opportunity. If so, students from poorer backgrounds could be helped in a variety of ways: they could receive a larger bursary (means tested on parental income); or they could be allowed more generous repayment terms; or universities could be paid a 'bounty' for recruiting certain types of student. These possibilities are discussed in section 6. Universities, too, could help such students, for instance by having higher tuition fees than otherwise, and using the additional revenue to assist poorer applicants.

Graduate students would be funded similarly. There would be bursaries for individual students, who would choose the supervisor best suited to their needs. The arrangements in particular institutions for ensuring that students made progress, and the details of completion rates should be published together with any relevant explanatory material.

The administration of bursaries   There is no necessity to depart from the present methods for the payment of grants and their reimbursement to local authorities. It is open to discussion whether local authorities should continue to meet ten per cent of the bill, but functioning simply as an agency they would minimise the administrative costs of the new system. Each term they would send the institution a cheque covering tuition fees and that element of maintenance which was being funded. Any surplus over fees would be made over to the student by way of a cheque. While not quite knave-proof, the system minimises the potential misapplication of funds which could result if the bursary were paid directly to the student.

5.3 Financing Capital and Funding Research

Tapering recurrent grants   The extent to which higher education can become largely independent of the state will depend both on the success of the government's efforts to induce more diversity in research funding and on a more active approach to fund raising. It will take time to build endowments, and so there is a strong case for tapering the direct grant over at least ten years, rather than removing it at once. Such a grant should be fixed in real terms, perhaps at a quarter or a fifth of the present income of a particular institution, and reduced at regular intervals. This grant should be used only to sustain research or to build endowments.

Further capital provision   Not all institutions are equally well placed in terms of their capital provision or their ability to create endowments. Recurrent funds were never intended to cover major capital projects, and the Joint Select Committee described earlier should undertake an early review of the capital provision of existing institutions in order to recommend the extent to which government should make further resources available. With the assistance of officials from the DES it would recommend priorities, but it would be for the Secretary of State to determine the annual building programme to accomplish such projects over a terms of years. Clearly he would have to account for his action/ inaction to Parliament, and the Joint Select Committee would no doubt comment. Reasonable professional fees would be included in such capital grants.

If, as is likely, the government favours the future expansion of higher education, further capital provision might be recommended by the Joint Select Committee, taking full account of the developing pattern of student choice and the bids made by individual institutions.

Funding research   There should be similar procedures where endowment is concerned once recurrent grants had ended. Where existing endowments are insufficient, the Joint Select Committee would be able to recommend that one-off grants, on a pound-for-pound or a more generous incentive basis, should be made to strengthen an institution's endowment. Again, the use of such endowments might be restricted, i.e. to basic research. Such funds might be channelled through the UFC (if retained) or the Research Councils.

The bulk of research funding should come by way of contracts from a diversity of sources including the Research Councils or their successors. There should be a continuing, if limited, role for the UFC in funding basic research for which no other provision was made; endowment income is not likely to be sufficient for large or risky projects. Imperfect as they are, the criteria by which such funds were allocated would have to be performance-related, and have some regard to the institution's success in attracting contract funding from a wide variety of sources.

Institutions could also include in their fee structure, once full freedom was obtained, a contribution towards the cost of basic research, since it is helpful to teaching. Such a contribution would be limited by competitive pressures, but in the case of the more prestigious institutions might be a useful additional source of research funds.

5.4 Implications of the System

Summary of the main features   The greater part of the funding of higher education would come from students, and it would be up to institutions to determine how many they took, the mix and, eventually, the charge they made. Potential students, intelligent and with multiple sources of advice readily available, are a highly sophisticated market force, particularly with the increased flow of information described earlier. Institutions would compete for these fee-paying students, and would necessarily be responsive and flexible to changing student preferences. A good loan system might well generate new forms of custom through innovations in teaching style and course provision.

Possibilities for government intervention   Government and other bodies would be able to influence choices by making available bursaries of various kinds for particular students. Such an approach reconciles the efficiency of market systems with a role for government policy and does so without detriment to academic autonomy.

The most obvious form of intervention is for government to offer more or larger bursaries in particular subjects. It would be open to other bodies such as commercial firms or the armed services to promote themselves by the provision of bursaries. Students who did not obtain a bursary might be allowed to qualify for a state loan, though that again could not be open-ended. Students seeking additional degree-level qualifications or further professional training, who must currently rely on non-mandatory awards should be brought within the loan scheme, even if they are not eligible for a bursary; and local authorities might consider giving some of their non-mandatory awards in the form of bursaries, supplemented by loans. In the longer term the government should consider whether its loan scheme should supplement or replace local authority discretionary awards.

There are many other examples. Shorter courses, could be encouraged by paying a higher annual bursary for them, making such students more attractive to higher education institutions. There could be special bursaries for retraining, and smaller bursaries for distance learning or external degrees. Similarly, the government could influence the supply side by offering a 'bounty' for each student of a particular type.

Government could take an even more active role. Suppose it were thought that the sort of scheme just described were too competitive for the world of learning. If so, there is a whole range of policies government could adopt within the famework suggested. One would be to ration out the state bursaries or at least to set a limit to the number of publicly-funded bursaries which any one institution could obtain, perhaps determined by reference to the number needed to maintain a viable institution. Such a system, however, would easily tend in the direction which led to the Education Reform Act. An alternative would be to supplement fee provision with a continued direct grant, though the grant should not exceed a relatively small fraction of the fee income of an institution. Dependency and direction would otherwise follow.

Perhaps the best method is a mechanism which conforms more closely with the logic of the proposed system. The starting point is to note the freedom of bodies other than the DES to fund bursaries either for fees and/or maintenance. It would be open, say, for the Scottish Office, concerned about the importance to the regional economy of a particular university, to create a number of bursaries tenable only at that university. The purpose of such bursaries would be explicit; and they would have to pass Treasury scrutiny, and would therefore not be subject to the normal doubts about concealed subsidy. Similarly, at postgraduate level there might be bursaries to study subjects of relevance to a particular department. Local government too, could create bursaries within the constraints of their financial set up. All such actions would be open to public scrutiny and debate in a way which is not possible with the present bureaucratic allocation of resources.

These examples bring out what is probably the single most important point — the proposals are consistent with *any* view of higher education. In a totally market-oriented system the only constraint on state bursaries would be their number; students would use them at their chosen institution; and institutions which failed to attract sufficient students would go to the wall. At the other end of the spectrum, all bursaries could be tied to specific institutions, perhaps even to specific subjects, thus mimicking the present set up. Our proposals are compatible with both extremes *and with anywhere along the spectrum in between.* The real debate should not be about the *idea* of bursaries, but about what proportion should (or should not) be tied to specific institutions and/or subjects.

The limitations to intervention   Such possibilities of government influence will attract criticism that the bursaries mechanism does nothing to reduce government interference with higher education. Critics of this sort see universities and polytechnics rather than government as giving student grants. It is true that grants automatically follow the award of a place, but the argument that universities are thereby in control overlooks a number of factors. Local authorities are constrained by legislation, whose shape and possible amendment are under the *de facto* control of government. The government's reluctance to raise fees suggests that they do not see this as the easiest way to control universities: under the 1988 Act control is imposed on higher education not through fees paid via the grant system, but through conditions attached to the direct grant by the UFC.

If government gave bursaries only to universities which accepted certain conditions, the reality would be no worse than under the new Act, but the politics would be very different. First, potential students and their parents would be unlikely to accept restrictions on their choices simply because the institutions concerned had not accepted the conditions which the government wished to impose. Second, the conditions would be drawn into public debate and would have to be seen as reasonable. Third, government bursaries would not be the sole source of student finance; with a satisfactory loan system, maintenance would no longer be dependent on a grant and, if its statutory basis were that proposed in section 4.3, loans could be used also to cover fees. Fourth, once the expectation was created that bursaries were linked to 'A' level performance, it would be difficult for the government to attach additional conditions. Finally, it is hard to see how it would be possible politically to move from the present system to bursaries if the latter were made in effect discretionary or subject to restrictive conditions.

All that is open to government is influence through the payment of more generous bursaries, and such measures would be subject to the need to convince the Treasury of their sense. Central to the argument is the belief that attempts at central planning are doomed to failure. This is a point which the Treasury is likely to latch on to, once its fears about open-endedness are removed.

Advantages of the strategy While the prime concern has been with the independence of higher education institutions and with the inevitable and damaging results of attempts to plan the system centrally, the system proposed here also encourages efficiency and accountability. It is wrong to think that it would restrict choice; it will make for greater choice although that is not the main argument in its favour. But there will inevitably be some students, as now, who cannot have what they want.

A major implication of these decentralised arrangements for higher education is the added power they give to the consumer, i.e. students. Whether or not this is an advantage depends on ones view of students' ability to make wise choices about institutions and courses, i.e. the issue of consumer information. Given the safeguards described earlier, we believe that students will make sensible choices, and all the more so if loans are national-insurance-based and so do not unduly bias their choice of degree or subsequent career. Most universities would prefer to live with the individual choices of many students than to leave decisions to a central planning agency.

The consequential advantage of the scheme is that universities would face a substantial incentive to teach properly. Under present arrangements an institution can increase neither its (home) student numbers nor its income from such students by teaching better; and the incentive faced by ambitious academics to focus their efforts on research rather than teaching is well known. Our proposals correct this imbalance.

Second, the scheme allows universities to manage their own affairs as they think best, and so encourages flexibility, innovation and diversity, a highly desirable state of affairs where consumers are well informed. The objection that responsiveness on the supply side will lead to continuous disruption is something of a straw man. There will certainly be changes in demand, but no reason why they should create new or insurmountable problems. Even if the pull of fashion were strong, well-run institutions would make a long-run commitment to expansion only when it was clear that there had been a lasting change in demand.

A third advantage is the added possibility of expanding the size and range of higher education. Bursaries should be available not only to mature students, but to all those in search of further professional training or second qualifications, replacing their non-mandatory grants. In addition it will be open to students without bursaries to take a degree, using the loan scheme to meet fees and maintenance. Such expansion is possible for little extra public expenditure once the loan scheme set out in section 4.3 is in place. It would be possible over time to replace *all* LEA non-mandatory awards, and the process could be speeded with some local authority pump priming. None of this is possible with commercial loans.

Fourth, the scheme encourages plural sources of funding, not only from government and private sources in the UK, but also from overseas. One implication is that universities would be free to charge whatever fees they wished. In consequence EC students would pay the same fees as UK and all other students, thus increasing non-Treasury funding sources for UK institutions of higher education, and this process could go even further if some variant of Patel's (1988) 'Euro-voucher' idea were adopted.

Fifth, the combination of bursaries and loans, if properly constructed, safeguards the position of poorer students; indeed, as discussed shortly, such a system could actually increase equality of opportunity.

Sixth, the specific organisation of the scheme can be made to suit different government perspectives without impairing the basic stability of the system. Thus a change of government will not be destabilising.

A further advantage of which academics will be conscious is that 'US-type' tenure, while not seriously impeding the ability of universities to manage themselves, genuinely protects the freedom of individuals.

Finally, and crucially, the system offers greater defences than any alternative against excessive interference by government. The major source of independence for institutions of higher education is the plurality of sources of funding. A second defence should not be overlooked, namely the political power of students as informed consumers if government were to attempt to go beyond acceptable limits in restricting the number of bursaries or constraining them to particular subjects or institutions.

In comparison with the present system, these arrangements have advantages in terms of efficiency, social justice and individual freedom. Perhaps for this reason the Secretary of State for Education, when the Education Reform Bill made its last appearance in the House of Commons, alluded in clearly sympathetic terms to the possibility of a future move towards decentralisation *(Hansard* (Commons), 19 July 1988, cols 988–9).

6 Some Specific Policy Proposals

6.1 The Range of Policy Choices

Table 2 attempts to draw together the threads of earlier discussion by setting out schematically the main ingredients of the system and the more important policy choices which can be made within it. The first part shows how universities will be financed (via students, via government and from other sources); the second shows the extent to which institutions of higher education will (or will not) be subject to regulation, in particular with respect to student numbers, conditions of employment and to the level of fees they may charge.

Since universities will be financed mainly by students the main part of the table concerns their sources of income, namely state bursaries, loans, and the private sector. Bursaries can come not only from the DES, but also from other state agencies, such as the police and the armed services. There are three policy decisions relevant to bursaries. First, their average size: should they cover only the average level of fees, or should they also make a contribution to the student's maintenance? Second, the variation in their size: bursaries would certainly have to be higher for science and medicine than for the arts; they could also be higher in the face of shortages in a particular skill; and they could be higher for students from poorer backgrounds. Third, would the bursaries be restricted either by subject (classics, Urdu), or by institution (e.g. usable only at Scottish universities)?

Loans, as we saw in section 4, can be organised in two ways. Income-related loans will generally be state-run, with repayment via the tax system or via National Insurance Contributions. Alternatively, loans can be organised along mortgage lines by the state, by the private sector or by the two sectors in combination, with or without a subsidised interest rate. In either case repayment could be required in full, or could be remitted in whole or in part if a student subsequently went into a particular job or came from a particular background.

The third major source of student income is the private sector. The most common items under this head are the student's own earnings; the student's past saving or inherited wealth; bank overdrafts and credit cards; support in cash or kind from the student's family, including rent-free accommodation; finance from the student's university (e.g. a scholarship or payment from a hardship fund); finance from industry (e.g. a bursary from British Telecom); and finance from overseas.

45

Table 2: ORGANISATION OF HIGHER EDUCATION: THE RANGE OF POLICY OPTIONS

FINANCE

- bursaries
  - average level
    - low (e.g. average fee only)
    - high (fee + some maintenance)
  - variation in size
    - higher for science than arts
    - higher for skill shortages
    - higher for poor students
  - restriction in use
    - to subject (e.g. classics)
    - to university (e.g. Scottish)

STUDENTS

- loans
  - income-related repayment (state loan)
    - method
      - income tax
      - Nat Ins Contribution
    - repayment
      - in full
      - depends on subsequent job
      - partial if student poor
  - mortgage repayment (state loan, private, or mixed)
    - interest rate
      - unsubsidised
      - subsidised
    - repayment
      - in full
      - depends on subsequent job
      - partial if student poor
- private sector
  - own earnings
  - past savings
  - credit card, etc
  - family
  - finance from university
  - finance from industry
  - finance from overseas

FINANCE (continued)

- GOV'T — DES
  - state bursaries
    - other dept's e.g. Scot. Office
    - local authority bursaries } see bursaries above
  - residual recurrent grant
  - ad hoc grants (e.g. for capital expenditure)
  - 'bounty' for particular students/subjects
  - research councils
  - specific gov't research contracts
- OTHER
  - entrepreneurial activity
  - industrial sponsorship
  - fund raising, appeals, etc

REGULATION

- DEGREE STRUCTURE
  - unrestricted, but subject to inspection
- STUDENT NUMBERS
  - unrestricted
  - maximum no. of state bursaries
- TERMS OF EMPLOYMENT
  - unrestricted
  - restricted (e.g. no tenure before 35)
- FEE LEVELS
  - unrestricted
  - within state-ordained limits centrally determined

Institutions of higher education will still receive some of their income directly from government. The DES may continue to pay a residual recurrent grant, at least for some universities, at least initially; the Department may also make ad hoc grants from time to time, e.g. for capital expenditure; and it might pay universities a per capita 'bounty' for students studying certain subjects or from a particular background. In addition, institutions are likely to receive at least some of their research funding from the Research Councils or a successor body and possibly also from specific research contracts direct from government departments.

Finally, institutions can derive income from a variety of other sources, such as their own entrepreneurial activity, sponsorship from industry and from fund raising, appeals and similar activities.

The last part of the table considers whether universities will be subject only to the constraint of their revenue-raising powers, or whether they will face additional restrictions. Degree structures, for the most part, will be left to institutions themselves to determine but subject to external inspection, not least for reasons of consumer information. Institutions should generally be free to determine student numbers, though possibly with restrictions as to the number of publicly-funded students any one institution might accept. They would also be free to set the terms and conditions of their employees, though government, if it wished, could impose restrictions, e.g. about minimum pension entitlement, or about the universities' freedom (or lack of it) to offer tenured contracts. Finally, and of considerable importance, is the issue of whether institutions are completely free to set their own fee levels, whether fees may vary only within a given range, or whether fee levels will be centrally established for all institutions of higher education.

6.2 Different Models of Higher Education

The options in the table make clear the diversity possible within the system proposed in section 5. Two issues predominate: how competitive should the higher education system be; and to what extent should its finance be redistributive? Intervention can take two forms: it can influence the *allocation* of resources (e.g. by subject or institution) and/or their *distribution* (e.g. towards poorer students). The proposals in section 5 are thus compatible with movements along two axes, one running from planned allocation to market allocation, and the other from less egalitarian to more egalitarian. This section illustrates the range of possibilities through two schemes, one a largely free market system with maximum competition and little redistribution, the other with fairly substantial intervention both educationally and to enhance equality of opportunity.

A nightwatchman model   Universities in this case are free to set their own fee levels, and the only constraint imposed by government on state bursaries is their total number and their monetary value. If the government did not wish to influence students' choice of subject all bursaries would have the same value; and one possible value is that of the average university tuition fee. The total number of such bursaries would be established by reference to political views about the efficient size of the higher education sector and the need to contain public expenditure.

Students would fund their maintenance from private sources, which would include their own earnings; assistance from family; and private philanthropy, including scholarships offered by institutions of higher education. In the interests of improving capital markets the state would probably wish to institute a commercial loan scheme. The government could offer loans itself out of public funds, or could act as guarantor to private lenders such as banks and building societies. In either case it would be possible to subsidise the interest rate.

A scheme of this sort has no redistributive implications except to the extent that the fee bursaries and any interest subsidies are paid out of progressive taxation. Poorer students would have to do more paid work; or they would have to find assistance from private sources; or they would go to a cheaper institution; or they would not attend higher education at all.

Research would be funded by the universities themselves, partly by building up endowments and partly through research contracts from industry. In addition government might fund specific projects which it wanted undertaken.

An interventionist model Government in this case has a 'hands on' approach. To influence the allocation of resources, some bursaries could be tied to vulnerable universities for reasons of regional balance, and others to subjects which the government wished to protect or promote. It might for example wish to protect certain arts subjects; or it might wish to encourage the expansion of a particular subject (e.g. engineering), to which end it could issue more and/or higher-valued tied bursaries.

The typical bursary would be large enough to pay tuition fees and to make a significant contribution to maintenance. Students with lower-income parents could receive a larger bursary. The total number and the size of bursaries would be decided on grounds of the efficient size of the higher education sector and also in terms of the needs of poorer students.

Students would be funded substantially by bursaries. The other main source of support would be a loan scheme with income-related repayments. Repayments would in any case be small for those who went into low paid jobs (nurses, primary school teachers), and hence would create little disincentive to going to university. It would, in addition, be open to government to exact smaller repayments from certain people (e.g. those going into certain jobs, or those coming from a particular background).

Such a scheme would be substantially redistributive. In a maximally redistributive scheme students from poor backgrounds would receive a bursary high enough to pay tuition and maintenance in full; and loans could be forgiven for those who subsequently went into (say) nursing.

Arrangements of this sort would increase the demand for higher education by poorer students. If it were wished in addition to operate on the supply side, universities could be paid a 'bounty' by government for any students from poorer backgrounds. A similar mechanism could be used for other groups which the government wished to encourage, e.g. mature students, or students studying a particular subject.

A further variant in this model concerns the ability of institutions to charge differential fees. Arguably, if the best institutions charge higher fees than others, the chances of students from poorer backgrounds will be restricted. To meet this point the government could establish fixed fees, with different levels for arts, science and medicine, leaving universities to compete in terms of quality of service and excellence of staff and teaching.

Alternatively, even in a maximally interventionist model, universities could be allowed to charge different fees (possibly within some range) with assistance for poorer students. Such assistance could take the form of higher bursaries, means tested on parental income; or there could be a higher 'bounty' to expensive universities for any poorer students they recruited; or the government could boost universities' scholarship funds (these methods are not mutually exclusive).

Research would be funded in part by higher education institutions themselves and by industry. Government in addition would fund research via specific research contracts and/or via the Research Councils or a successor body. It would also be possible for a residual recurrent grant to be retained both to fund research and to help reduce tuition fees.

We have two proposals to commend to the government, and to Vice-Chancellors and Principals, our academic colleagues, parents and students. First, we urge acceptance and speedy implementation of the specific National-Insurance-based loan scheme set out in section 4.3. Second, we recommend acceptance in principle of the system of financing and organising higher education described in section 5. Once the idea is accepted, a second stage is to debate the specific scheme to be implemented. At present we seek agreement only on the general system.

Notes

[1] The theory of market efficiency with and without state intervention, and the application of the theory to health care, education, housing and cash benefits, is discussed in detail in Barr (1987). The basic theory is discussed in Ch. 4, section 3, and the whole argument is set out for non-economists in the non-technical appendix to Ch. 4. For specific discussion of the NHS, see Chs 12 and 13, and Barr, Glennerster and Le Grand (1988).

[2] Neither of us had the remotest idea earlier this year to what extent we would set aside our other research to concentrate on the Education Reform Bill. Had our contracts been tightly and rigidly specified this paper, amongst others, would not have been written. We, at least, think that would have been a pity.

[3] For an account of the £10 million loan to University College, Cardiff and the grilling of both the Department of Education and Science and the UGC by the Public Accounts Committee, see David Gow's article 'The Road from Rack and Ruin', *The Guardian,* 17 May 1988, p. 25.

[4] This section is based, almost in its entirety, on ideas suggested to us by Mervyn King.

[5] The first explicit proposal in a British context was by Prest (1966); see also Blaug (1966), Glennerster, Merrett and Wilson (1968) and Robbins' (1980, pp. 31–7) account of his conversion to loans. The literature is surveyed by Blaug (1970) and systems elsewhere discussed by Woodhall (1978) and Blaug and Woodhall (1979). For recent discussion see Glennerster (1981) and Farmer and Barrell (1982).

References

Arrow, K (1975), 'Vertical Integration and Communication' *Bell Journal of Economics,* Vol. 6, No. 1, pp. 173–83.

Ashworth, J (1982), 'Reshaping Higher Education in Britain', *Journal of the Royal Society of Arts.* October.

Barr, N A (1987), *The Economics of the Welfare State,* London: Weidenfeld and Nicolson.

Barr, N A, Glennerster, H and Le Grand, J (1988), 'Improving the National Health Service', in *Resourcing the National Health Service,* House of Commons Social Services Committee, Memoranda laid before the Committee, Session 1987–88, HC 264–IV, HMSO, London.

Barr, N A and Low, W (1988), *Students Grants and Student Poverty,* Discussion Paper No. 28, Welfare State Programme, London School of Economics.

Blaug, M (1966), 'Loans for Students?', *New Society,* 6 October, pp. 538–9.

Blaug, M (1967), 'Approaches to Educational Planning', *Economic Journal,* June.

Blaug, M (1970), *An Introduction to the Economics of Education,* Penguin.

Blaug, M (1980), 'Student Loans and the NUS', *Economic Affairs,* October, pp. 45–6.

Blaug, M (1987), *The Economics of Education and the Education of an Economist,* Edward Elgar.

Blaug, M, and Woodhall, M (1979), 'Patterns to Subsides to Higher Education in Europe', *Higher Education,* September, pp. 331–63, reprinted in Blaug (1987).

Brown, R G S (1970), *The Administrative Process in Britain,* Methuen.

Buchanan, J M, and Tullock, G (1962), *The Calculus of Consent,* University of Michigan Press, Ann Arbor.

Cyert, R M, and March, J G (1963), *A Behavioural Theory of the Firm,* Prentice-Hall.

Dearborn, D C, and Simon, H A (1958), 'Selective Perception: a Note on the Departmental Identification of Executives', *Sociometry,* Vol. 21, pp. 140–4.

Farmer, M and Barrell, R (1982), 'Why Student Loans are Fairer than Grants', *Public Money,* Vol. 2, No. 1, pp. 19–24.

Ferns, H S (1969), *Towards an Independent University,* Institute of Economic Affairs.

Ferns, H S (1982), *How Much Freedom for Universities?,* Institute of Economic Affairs.

Glennerster, H (1981), 'Role of the State in Financing Recurrent Education: Lessons from European Experience', in Bowman, M (ed.), *Collective Choice in Education,* Kluwer and Nijhoff.

Glennerster, H, Merrett, S and Wilson, G (1968), 'A Graduate Tax', *Higher Education Review,* Vol. 1, No. 1.

Griffith, J (1987), *The Attack on Higher Education,* Council for Academic Freedom and Democracy.

Hills, G (1983), 'Developing Individually', *Times Higher Education Supplement,* 3 June.

Hills, G (1988), 'Education for the Enterprising', *Scottish Enterprise Culture: a Radical Reaffirmation,* Cooper and Lybrand Gleneagles Conference.

Hills, G and Kelly, A (1988), 'An Alternative Funding Scheme for Higher Education', submission to the CVCP Working Group on the Finance of Higher Education.

Jackson, P M (1982), *The Political Economy of Bureaucracy,* Philip Allan.

Kedourie, E (1988), *Diamonds into Glass,* Centre for Policy Studies.

Kogan, M and Kogan, D (1982), *The Attack on Higher Education,* Kogan Page.

Krupp, S (1961), *Pattern in Organisational Analysis,* Holt, Rinehart and Winston.

Lawrence, P R, and Lorsch, J W (1967), *Organisation and Environment,* Graduate School of Economics, Harvard University, Cambridge, Mass.

Layard, P R G (1972), 'Economic Theories of Educational Planning', in Peston, M, and Corry, B (eds), *Essays in Honour of Lord Robbins,* Weidenfeld and Nicolson.

Leibenstein, H (1966), 'Allocative Efficiency versus X-Efficiency', *American Economic Review,* Vol. 56, June, pp. 392–415.

Leibenstein, H (1973), 'Competition and X-Efficiency: a Reply', *Journal of Political Economy,* Vol. 81.

Loasby, B J (1976), *Choice, Complexity and Ignorance,* Cambridge University Press.

March, J G, and Olsen, J P (1976), *Ambiguity and Choice in Organisations,* Bergen.

March, J G, and Simon, H A (1958), *Organisations,* Wiley, New York.

Moore, A, and Roberts, G (1988), *A Consumer's Guide to Student Finance,* Telegraph Publications.

Moser, C A and Layard, P R G (1964), 'Planning the Scale of Higher Education in Britain: Some Statistical Problems', *Journal of the Royal Statistical Society,* December, pp. 473–513, and Discussion, *ibid.,* pp. 513–526.

Patel, I G (1988), 'Exporting Education', *The Independent,* 25 July 1988, p. 19.

Peacock, A T (1986), 'Buckingham's Fight for Independence', *Economic Affairs,* February/March.

Peacock, A T and Wiseman, J (1964), *Education for Democrats,* Institute for Economic Affairs.

Prest, A R (1966), *Financing University Education,* Institute for Economic Affairs.

Pfeffer, J, Salancik, G R, and Leblebici, H (1976), 'Personal Influences in Organisational Decision Making', *Administrative Science Quarterly,* Vol. 21, pp. 227–45.

Robbins, L C (1980), *Higher Education Revisited,* Macmillan.

Shackle, G S (1974), 'Decision: the Human Predicament', *Annals of the American Academy of Political and Social Sciences,* Vol. 412, March, pp. 1–10.

Simon, H A (1957), *Models of Man,* Harper and Row, New York.

Underwood, S (forthcoming), *Administrative Lessons from Student Loans in the USA,* York University.

UK (1960), *Grants to Students* (the Anderson Report), Report of the Committee Appointed by the Minister of Education and the Secretary of State for Scotland, Cmnd 1051, HMSO, London.

UK (1963), *Higher Education* (the Robbins Report), Cmnd. 2154, HMSO, London.

UK (1967), *Select Committee on Public Accounts*, Session 1966/7, HMSO, London.

UK (1982), *Select Committee on Education and Science*, Session 1981/82, HMSO, London.

Williamson, O (1971), 'Managerial Discretion, Organisation Form and the Multi-Division Hypothesis', in Marris, R, and Wood, A (eds), *The Corporate Economy*, Macmillan.

Williamson, O (1975), *Markets and Hierarchies: Analysis and Anti-Trust Implications*, Free Press.

Woodhall, M (1978), *Review of Student Support Schemes in Selected OECD Countries*, Paris: OECD.

THE DAVID HUME INSTITUTE

The David Hume Institute was established as a company limited by guarantee in January 1985, and it is registered as a charity. Its registration number in Scotland is 91239.

The objects of the Institute are to promote discourse and research on the economic and legal aspects of public policy questions.

Honorary President (1988–1991) Judge Thijmen Koopmans, Court of Justice of the European Communities
Chairman Sir Gerald Elliot FRSE
Executive Director Professor Sir Alan Peacock FBA
Secretary and Treasurer H L Snaith

Registered Office, 10 Hope Street, Charlotte Square,
Edinburgh EH2 4DD
Tel: 031 225 6298

HUME PAPERS
1   Banking Deregulation *Michael Fry*
2   Reviewing Industrial Aid Programmes:
    (1) The Invergordon Smelter Case *Alex Scott and Margaret Cuthbert*
3   Sex at Work: Equal Pay and the "Comparable Worth" Controversy *Peter Sloane.*
4   The European Communities' Common Fisheries Policy: A Critique *Antony W Dnes*
5   The Privatisation of Defence Supplies *Gavin Kennedy*
6   The Political Economy of Tax Evasion *David J Pyle*
7   Monopolies, Mergers and Restrictive Practices: UK Competition Policy 1948–87 *E Victor Morgan*

Published by **Aberdeen University Press**
8   The Small Entrepreneurial Firm Gavin C Reid and Lowell R Jacobsen
9   How Should Health Services be Financed? Allan Massie
10 Strategies for Higher Education — The Alternative White Paper John Barnes and Nicholas Barr

SUNTORY TOYOTA INTERNATIONAL CENTE FOR ECONOMICS AND RELATED DISCIPLINES

ST/ICERD was established in 1978 on the basis of funds donated to the London School of Economics by Suntory Ltd. and the Toyota Motor Company Limited of Japan. It is the largest research centre at LSE, acting as a "research council" within the School, awarding funds on the basis of competitive peer review to finance a wide variety of research by members of the School staff, both inside and outside the Centre. It also provides funds for the LSE Suntory-Toyota public lectures and a variety of seminars in different fields. It produces discussion papers on a wide variety of subjects which are distributed free of charge. Eleven Occasional Papers have been produced to date, which are for sale from the Centre. Support for postgraduate students is offered annually in the form of studentships. In addition, the Centre is host to academic visitors from all over the world, and provides accommodation and facilities for research programmes supported by the ESRC and other funding agencies.

OCCASIONAL PAPERS

1 The Economics of the Professions (1982) by Patrick Foley, Avner Shaked, John Sutton
  A guide to the literature with over 100 items, with introductory essay and full cross references
2 Panel Data on Incomes (1983) Edited by A B Atkinson and F A Cowell
  A selection of papers presented at a Conference held in June, 1982 on the Analysis of Panel Data on Incomes
3 Confucianism and Taoism (1984) by Max Weber, abridged by M Morishima. Translated by M Alter and J Hunter
  A new translation of Weber's treatise on Chinese religions
4 Homeless in London, 1971–81 (1984) by Helen Austerberry, Kerry Schott, Sophie Watson
  An analysis of the impact of the severe housing crisis in London — arising from the cutback in housing expenditure — on the different types of households most affected by it
5 Regionalisation in France, Italy and Spain (1984) Edited by M Hebbert and H Machin
  Papers arising from a seminar held in June 1983 on nation–region conflicts in economic policy-making

6   Unemployment Benefits and Unemployment Duration (1985) by
    A B Atkinson and J Micklewright
    Drawing on a sample of unemployed men in the UK in the 1970s, this
    study challenges the popular perception that the benefit system
    provides generous insurance and other support.
7   The Economics of Soviet Arms (1985) by Peter Wiles and Moshe
    Efrat
    Part I is concerned with military expenditures in domestic rubles; Part
    II is about the economics of the Soviet Arms trade with the Third
    World
8   The Evolution of Central Banks (1985) by C A E Goodhart
    This book seeks to establish, using analytical arguments and historical
    example, how the evolution of Central Banks occurred, and how far it
    was a natural development in response to revealed needs
9   Paying for Pensions: the French Experience (1985) by Tony Lynes
    This study traces the history of developments in France's pension
    provision, culminating in the government's decision to reduce the
    pension age from 65 to 60 in 1983
10 Tax Benefit Models (1987) Edited by A B Atkinson and H Sutherland
    This is a collection of papers describing the research underlying the
    construction of tax-benefit models, with illustrations of their use.
11 How Tokyo Grows: Land Development and Planning on the
    Metropolitan Fringe (1988) by Michael Hebbert and Norihiro Nakal
    An analysis of the mechanisms of urban land development in Japan
    and a review of current policy measures

The Centre also produces discussion papers in the following subjects:
Economics, Theoretical Economics, International Economics, Econo-
metrics, International Studies, Japanese Studies, Comparative Industrial
Relations and Information Technology. These are all available, free of
charge, from Ruth Singh, (Room R411, 01-405-7686 ext. 3025).